THE
LITTLE BOOK OF
WORLD
MYTHOLOGY

HANNAH BOWSTEAD

summersdale

THE LITTLE BOOK OF WORLD MYTHOLOGY

An Hachette UK Company
www.hachette.co.uk

Summersdale Publishers Ltd
Part of Octopus Publishing Group Limited
Carmelite House
50 Victoria Embankment
LONDON
EC4Y 0DZ
UK

www.summersdale.com

Printed and bound in Poland

ISBN: 978-1-80007-176-6

Substantial discounts on bulk quantities of Summersdale books are available to corporations, professional associations and other organizations. For details contact general enquiries: telephone: +44 (0) 1243 771107 or email: enquiries@summersdale.com.

CONTENTS

INTRODUCTION

What is a myth? Is it an entertaining story, a historical account, an origin story, a teaching aid, a foundation for a belief or a cultural unifier? Yes!

The word *myth* derives from the Ancient Greek word *mythos*, meaning "story" or "narrative". But myths are more than fiction. They attempt to answer the big questions of life, death and the world around us, relating the exploits of gods and heroes to help us make sense of our own lives and relationships. These narratives can also provide a moral code, rich traditions and a sense of community and pride.

This book isn't a comprehensive guide to world mythology, not least because sources are patchy at best.

The forces of time, war, colonialism and oppression have tried their hardest to eradicate many mythologies. Luckily, they haven't been 100 per cent successful.

Instead, this book is an introduction to the mythologies of some of the world's greatest cultures, a whistle-stop tour which begins in the Ancient Middle East and travels through Europe, Asia, America and Oceania. Along the way you'll encounter warriors and tricksters, monsters and spirits, love, loss, war, sex and even a divine striptease. Enjoy the ride.

MIDDLE EAST

The civilizations and mythologies of the Middle East are *old*. As in, 3100 BCE old.

Ancient Mesopotamia was a region of Asia situated on the Tigris and Euphrates rivers, where Iraq and parts of Turkey, Iran, Syria and Kuwait are located today. Indeed, the name itself means "between the rivers", derived from the Greek words *mesos* (middle) and *potamos* (river – this also gives the hippopotamus its name). Mesopotamia was home to a number of civilizations, including Sumer and Akkad, which flourished from before the beginning of recorded history (around 3000 BCE) until the fall of Babylon in 539 BCE.

Mesopotamian civilizations are some of the oldest in the world, and are duly credited with some of humanity's most significant developments, such as crop planting, advances in mathematics and astronomy and, oh, the invention of the wheel. Mesopotamia is also known for its literature, including the epic of Gilgamesh, considered the world's oldest surviving story, which was only deciphered in the late nineteenth century.

Almost-neighbouring Egypt has achieved much greater fame in the modern world. Evoking images of mummies, sphinxes and terrific winged eyeliner, Egyptian civilization has found a loving home in the hearts of excited children and archaeologists alike. But condensing such a long-lasting (approximately 3100–30 BCE) and complex civilization down to a few scarab beetles and Eyes of Horus runs the risk of belittling and conflating Egypt's achievements. After all, Cleopatra lived closer to you, now, reading this book, than to the building of the Great Pyramid of Giza.

Ancient Egyptian civilization flourished thanks to its location on the banks of the life-giving River Nile, whose yearly flooding allowed the Egyptians to develop a stable system of agriculture to support the population.

Ancient Egypt is, of course, famed for its architecture and construction techniques – the Great Pyramid of Giza being the oldest of the Seven Wonders of the Ancient World, and the only one still standing. The legacy of Ancient Egypt also includes its medicine, literature and striking art.

MESOPOTAMIAN MYTHOLOGY

The myths of Mesopotamian civilizations which have survived in the present day came to us on stone or clay tablets, written in cuneiform, one of the planet's oldest writing systems. These tales, considered to be the earliest works of literature in the world, explore the creation of the world, the adventures of heroes, and humans' dependence on the gods, themes held in common with countless other mythologies.

You might never have heard of Mesopotamia, the Sumerians or the Akkadians, but echoes of their myths have cascaded through the centuries and nestled in the myths and tales of subsequent civilizations. Many of the themes and elements explored in the following pages (immortality, destruction and rebirth, divine right to rule) can be found in other religious texts such as the Bible, and may well have served as inspiration for the myths of Egypt, Greece and plenty more.

So, the stories and themes presented here may be more familiar than you might have expected.

THE CIVILIZATIONS OF MESOPOTAMIA

Sumer was the earliest of the civilizations in Mesopotamia, and one of the oldest civilizations in the world. It emerged between the sixth and fifth millennium BCE. The Sumerians gave us the cuneiform writing script and also Gilgamesh, who you'll meet shortly.

Akkad was the central city of the Akkadian Empire, which arose in the third millennium BCE after the dominance of Sumer. Speakers of Sumerian and Akkadian were united under one empire.

Assyria was a northern Mesopotamian kingdom that lasted from around 2500 BCE until its fall between 612 and 609 BCE. Part of the Akkadian Empire until its collapse, Assyria then became one of two major Akkadian-speaking nations that rose out of the Akkadian Empire.

Babylonia was the other major nation that grew out of the collapse of the Akkadian Empire. Its central city was Babylon, home of the Hanging Gardens of Babylon, one of the Seven Wonders of the Ancient World.

GODS OF MESOPOTAMIA

Let's meet our first pantheon. A pantheon, put simply, is a set of gods – the word is Greek in origin and means "all gods". Like many pantheons, the Mesopotamian gods' names and relationships vary from source to source, making them tricky to untangle. But here goes.

The pantheon begins with Ki, the earth goddess, and An, the sky god (earth-mother and sky-father pairings are *really* common in mythology). Ki and An have various children, depending on who you ask, but these include Enlil, the air god, and Ninlil, the air goddess. Enki, the god of water and mischief, is said to be the son of An and his mistress Nammu. Ninlil and Enlil get together and produce the moon god Nanna, while Enki pairs with his sister Ningikuga to beget Ningal the moon goddess. Nanna and Ningal in turn are the parents of the sun god Utu and the love goddess Inanna.

Together, An, Enlil, Enki, Nanna, Utu, Inanna and another goddess called Ninhursag are known as the seven great gods. Phew.

ENUMA ELISH

The *Enuma Elish* is the name given to the creation myth of the Babylonians. The story starts with the creation of the universe from the primordial beings Apsu and Tiamat (some describe Tiamat as the embodiment of chaos, or a chaos dragon, which is just so metal). Next, all the gods were created, but Tiamat loathed the noise and commotion they produced (honestly, same), so Apsu decided to destroy them all.

Ea (another name for Enki – the god of water and mischief) heard about this plan and was not a fan. So he killed Apsu and created a son called Marduk from Apsu's heart. In retaliation, everyone's favourite chaos dragon Tiamat vowed to fight Marduk and avenge Apsu.

The fight was vicious, but eventually Marduk pierced Tiamat's heart with an arrow, and she was defeated. He split her body in two to create the sky and the earth. In rapid succession, Marduk created the constellations, the calendar, night, day, the moon, the clouds, rain and, finally, humans. The city of Babylon was constructed in his honour.

THE GREAT FLOOD

A recurring narrative in Mesopotamian mythology is the humankind-destroying flood. For those who know the biblical story of Noah, these will sound familiar.

Atra-Hasis is the Akkadian version. Enki had the bright idea to create humans to do all the gods' hard labour for them. But the humans got busy and overpopulation quickly became a problem, so Enlil decided to send a great flood. Wanting to save his beloved humans, Enki instructed our hero Atra-Hasis to build a boat to escape the waters. Enlil was livid at Enki for ruining his fun, but they eventually put their differences aside and devised some other methods for population control: death, stillbirth and celibacy.

Eridu Genesis is the Sumerian version. The story is similar to Atra-Hasis (as far as anyone can tell – the tablet it survives on is in pieces). Again the gods created humans and again they pulled a sharp U-turn and sent a destructive flood. The hero, Ziusudra, built a boat at Enki's behest and survived the flood to preserve humankind.

THE EPIC OF GILGAMESH

The epic of Gilgamesh is considered the world's oldest known story. Its eponymous hero Gilgamesh was the (probably real-life) king of the Sumerian city Uruk. But he was arrogant, greedy and cruel, so the gods sent an adversary, Enkidu, to rein him in. However, Gilgamesh and Enkidu hit it off, embarking on some jolly monster hunting together. The bromance abruptly ended when Enkidu was killed by the gods, forcing Gilgamesh to confront his own mortality. He set out to discover the secret of eternal life.

On his journey Gilgamesh met the immortal man Utnapishtim and asked him how he escaped death. Utnapishtim explained that Enki had warned him about a coming flood (sound familiar?), so he'd built a boat to house his family, animals and plants. After a week of violent rain, Utnapishtim released three birds, the last of which failed to return, signalling that dry land was finally nearby.

After hearing this, Gilgamesh returned to Uruk wiser and happier, at last accepting his own mortality because humankind as a whole would always survive.

ADAPA AND THE SOUTH WIND

Mortality is a recurrent theme in Mesopotamian myth, as we have seen with Gilgamesh. But where did mortality come from and why is it that all humans must die? One mythological explanation is the story of Adapa.

Adapa had been gifted with immeasurable intelligence by Enki (sometimes thought to be his father). One day when Adapa was out fishing, the South Wind – a winged figure – flew down and caused Adapa's boat to capsize. Adapa lashed out in anger and snapped the South Wind's wings right off.

The supreme god An summoned Adapa to heaven to face what he had done. Before Adapa left, Enki warned him not to eat any food or drink that the gods offered him. However, impressed by Adapa's intelligence, An had a change of heart and offered Adapa food that would grant him immortality. But obedient daddy's boy Adapa refused the offering, unwittingly condemning himself and the rest of humankind to mortal lives.

And so we now suffer disease and death. Thanks very much, Adapa.

WORSHIP AND PRACTICE

The myths of Mesopotamia asserted that humans were created by the gods to serve the gods, so proper worship and reverence should be shown to them. Prayer and omen interpretation seem to have been common practices, if the surviving texts are anything to go by. The Mesopotamians also carried out rituals: for example, at each new year the Babylonians held a ritualistic reading of the *Enuma Elish*.

These myths weren't just the foundation for Mesopotamian religion and customs, but also their politics. Cities would have patron deities, such as Marduk for Babylon. The earliest kings in these myths were directly descended from the gods – for example, Gilgamesh is described as being semi-divine – and later Mesopotamian rulers would have used this ancestry to justify their kingship and place themselves on a higher plane than their "ordinary" subjects. We'll see something similar again shortly with the Egyptians.

∽ EGYPTIAN MYTHOLOGY ∾

Egyptian mythology has come to us in fragments from hymns, temple decorations and other religious texts. These myths formed the backbone of Egyptian religion and culture, offering explanations for how the world came to be and why it is the way it is. They share many themes with Mesopotamian mythology, such as death, rebirth and eternal life.

A core concept to Egyptian mythology is the constant struggle between order and chaos, embodied by the principle of Ma'at, which we'll explore in more detail later on. In the cycles of nature and time, these struggles to maintain balance and order are repeated time and time again, and it was up to the pharaoh to keep chaos in check. This connected him with the Egyptian gods whose job this had previously been.

In the following pages, we've got some Egyptian big hitters - names you might have heard of like Osiris, Anubis and Horus - as well as a chaos snake and a drunk lion goddess. Plenty to love.

THE ENNEAD

The Ennead was a set of nine gods worshipped at Heliopolis, a major Egyptian city and religious centre. They're some of the best-known Egyptian gods today.

The sun god Atum (also known as Ra) created himself – as you do – from the primordial waters. He spat, or maybe ejaculated (it's surprisingly unclear), and brought forth two children: Tefnut, goddess of rain, and Shu, god of air. Brother and sister then got together, resulting in two grandchildren for Atum: the earth god Geb, and the sky goddess Nut, who was adorned with twinkling stars and lifted up to arch over her brother. Geb and Nut also had children together, begetting the four remaining Ennead deities: Osiris, Isis, Set and Nephthys.

Osiris was the god of agriculture, the underworld and the dead. He coupled with his sister Isis. That left Set, god of storms and violence (sounds fun, doesn't he?), to pair off with Nephthys, goddess of death and darkness and the ultimate goth queen.

And Atum ruled as Egypt's first pharaoh.

MA'AT

Key to Egyptian mythology, religion and culture was the idea of balance, justice and cosmic order. This principle was called Ma'at, and it was a moral guide by which Egyptians were supposed to live. It was the pharaoh's job to uphold Ma'at and prevent chaos and disorder. Many stories from Egyptian myth came to represent this constant struggle between order and disorder. We'll encounter a few examples.

Ma'at was also the name for the goddess who personified the principle. Her main role was to judge the souls of the dead. When you died, your heart was weighed on a set of scales against a feather belonging to Ma'at. If your heart was lighter than the feather, you'd lived a good and principled life and could spend eternity in the paradise Aaru. If your heart was heavier than Ma'at's feather, however, all you had to look forward to was being devoured by the demoness Ammit, followed by eternal damnation in the underworld, which was called the Duat. A serious Ma'atter indeed.

THE ASCENSION OF RA

Ra (aka Atum) was Egypt's first pharaoh and the ultimate upholder of Ma'at. But he discovered that the humans were plotting to overthrow him. Total annihilation was obviously the solution, but instead of sending a flood like the Mesopotamians, Ra sent his daughter, Hathor.

Hathor took the form of Sekhmet, a bloodthirsty, lion-headed, fire-breathing warrior goddess, who killed thousands of humans in a frenzied rage. Ra decided enough was enough and ordered her to stop, but Sekhmet was enjoying herself too much and could not be controlled.

So Ra ordered for obscene quantities of beer to be mixed with red dye, and poured it over the plains. Sekhmet, mistaking the beer for a pool of blood, downed it and became roaring drunk. She passed out, awaking as the peaceful Hathor once more.

Ra was, understandably, sick of everything. Handing the rule of Egypt to Osiris, he ascended to the highest heavens, as far away from the humans as possible. Now the fallen humans must maintain Ma'at by themselves.

THE SUN GOD AND THE CHAOS SNAKE

Every day, Ra rose into the sky in his sun boat and brought light and life to all Egypt. And every sunset, Ra's boat would dip below the horizon and enter into the Duat. There, Ra would be met by Apep, a monstrous serpent who sought to destroy Ra and prevent sunrise, thus throwing Ma'at out of balance.

So every night, Ra fought with Apep. But Ra would not have to fight alone. Members of the Ennead often accompanied Ra in his boat on the journey through the Duat, including Set, who drove his spear through the chaos snake Apep and slayed him. But Apep could never be completely destroyed, and, the following night, he was there to greet Ra once more.

Yes, the serpent could never be truly defeated. But neither could Ra. For he would emerge from the Duat every morning and the sun would once again rise into the sky. With each passing day, Ma'at would be maintained and the cycles of death and rebirth would endure.

THE DEATH OF OSIRIS

Osiris, having inherited the kingship, had now become the ruler of Egypt, maintaining order, balance and righteousness with his wife Isis by his side. But it wasn't long before Osiris' eye wandered, and he had an affair with his sister Nephthys. The result of this was Anubis, the jackal-headed god of the underworld and inventor of embalming.

Nephthys' husband (and Osiris' brother) Set was enraged and enacted the ultimate revenge: he murdered Osiris. It isn't clear exactly how the murder was carried out, but one version has Set cutting Osiris' body into as many as 42 pieces and scattering them far and wide across the Egyptian world.

Devastated by her husband's death, Isis enlisted the help of her sister Nephthys (who presumably went behind her husband Set's back), and the two sisters set out together to recover Osiris' body. As the search dragged on and on, Isis' tears of mourning overflowed and caused the Nile river to flood, thus setting the precedent for the river's annual flooding.

OSIRIS REBORN

At long last, Isis and Nephthys found all the pieces of Osiris' body. Now what? Osiris was still, after all, dead. But the two sisters could count on the assistance of Anubis, master embalmer, and Thoth, god of wisdom and science. Together, the four deities pieced Osiris together like a jigsaw puzzle, embalmed him and wrapped him in linen cloths. This was the first ever mummification.

The gods waited with bated breath. Then Osiris' body gave a great shudder and sat up – Osiris was alive! Isis was overjoyed to be reunited with her beloved husband and, wasting no time, made love to him furiously. But Osiris' resurrection was only temporary, and he was bound to descend to the underworld, Duat, and become ruler of the dead.

To the Egyptians, Osiris' death and resurrection was a promise of eternal life. They believed that, if the correct funeral rites like mummification were carried out, each of them could be granted immortality in the afterlife, just like Osiris.

HORUS

When we left Isis, she'd just had a rollicking good time with Osiris. And, in due course, she gave birth to a falcon-headed son, Horus.

Following the murder of Osiris, Horus and Set became embroiled in a fierce struggle for kingship of Egypt. Set attempted to impregnate Horus with his seed, but Horus tossed the semen into a nearby river. In retaliation, Horus spread his own seed on some lettuce leaves, which Set promptly ate.

Then Horus lopped off Set's testicles. Set responded by gouging out one of Horus' eyes (this Eye of Horus would become an important emblem of all-seeing protection). And so on, and so on, in a seemingly never-ending battle between chaos and order that pushed Ma'at ever further out of reach.

Eventually, Horus was victorious and took his place as pharaoh. As direct descendant of Atum, one of the most important Egyptian deities, Horus became the spiritual force behind the pharaohs. Each new pharaoh had a little bit of Horus inside them, giving them the divine right to rule.

CENTRAL EUROPE

The Ancient Greeks and Romans were natural storytellers. Indeed, many consider the Greeks (in particular Homer) responsible for the birth of Western literature, and the Romans were eager to build on this legacy. Their mythologies are accordingly grand – and super fun.

The vibrant body of Greek mythology features the 12 all-star Olympian gods, their predecessors the Titans, and their messy encounters, in all their glory, with ordinary mortals. These myths explained creation and natural phenomena, extolled the exploits of superstar heroes like Heracles and Achilles, and explored the origins of Greek culture and customs.

Greek gods helped to make sense of the arbitrary and chaotic nature of life: if you drowned in a shipwreck, it was because you'd forgotten to make adequate sacrifices to Poseidon. Whoops. The Greek gods were an awful lot like humans: temperamental, hot-headed, jealous and constantly bickering, so naturally a world run by them would be, well, a bit all over the place.

Greek mythology had enormous influence over the arts and literature of its time, and still does in today's Western world - even if you haven't seen *Troy* or Disney's *Hercules*, you'll probably have learned about the Oedipus complex or accidentally downloaded a Trojan Horse virus. These ancient stories still resonate with us today.

It's easy to think that Roman mythology basically asked to copy the Greeks' homework and the Greeks said, "Sure, but change it up so it's not obvious." Many of the same characters and stories reappear, with different names or variations, and the Romans repurposed and expanded these tales.

But it's unfair to say the Romans simply stole their mythology from the Greeks - although they did really, *really* want to be as cool as them. As the Roman Empire expanded, so did its pantheon. Instead of forbidding the gods of the cultures they'd conquered, the Romans assimilated them into their existing religion. What results is a rich tapestry that interweaves mythological elements from Greece and other cultures with Roman tales and morals.

GREEK MYTHOLOGY

The Ancient Greeks were a busy lot. Ancient Greek civilization began around the twelfth century BCE and lasted for hundreds of years, during which time the Greeks devised and developed such things as democracy, literature, philosophy, drama, poetry, science and art. So, not much. Suffice to say, Greek civilization involved a lot of writing and a lot of fighting, a lot of thinking and a *lot* of drinking.

Greek mythology is similarly complex. These stories are often messy, and there's no consistent system of morality or justice. Human characters' lives are at the mercy of the gods' whims and fancies. If terrible things happened to you, it's not necessarily because you deserved them, but because Hera or Apollo did or didn't take a shine to you.

Of course, only selected greatest hits are covered here: the Titans and Olympians, a sprinkling of heroes and the Trojan War. But this is the exciting part. If these stories whet your appetite for Greek mythology, there is still *so much* to discover.

THE TITANS

It all began with Chaos, and out of Chaos sprang Gaia, Mother Earth. She in turn gave life to a son: Ouranos. Mother and son came together (here we go again) and produced 12 robust children. These were the Titans.

The youngest Titan was Kronos, and he fancied Ouranos' power for himself. So, taking his great stone sickle that Gaia had made, he castrated his father, and flung his genitals into the ocean. Easy as pie. Kronos took the throne of heaven with his wife (and sister) Rhea by his side.

But uneasy was the head that wore the crown. Kronos suspected that his children would overthrow him just as he had overthrown his father. So each time Rhea gave birth, Kronos took the child and ate it. This happened five times, and Rhea was, understandably, not thrilled. So next time, she handed Kronos a stone instead of her infant son, and Kronos – without pausing to examine this stone-baby – swallowed it whole.

And so Rhea's sixth child survived. His name? Zeus.

THE OLYMPIANS

All grown up now, Zeus wanted revenge. He forced Kronos to vomit up his two brothers and three sisters. And the stone. The siblings joined together to overthrow Kronos in a terrible war called the Titanomachy. After their victory, Zeus and Co. moved to Mount Olympus (hence "Olympians"), where Zeus became king of the gods and ruler of the universe.

Hera is both Zeus' sister and wife, making her the queen of the gods. She is the goddess of marriage and childbirth, but it is her vengeful jealousy that she's best known for.

Poseidon is the god of the sea, carrying his mighty trident and commanding the waves and storms. Demeter is a bit more chill, ruling over nature and agriculture. And Hestia is the goddess of the hearth, home and family.

And then there's the goth of the family, Hades. As ruler of the underworld (also called Hades, just to confuse us), Hades doesn't live on Olympus and isn't considered an Olympian. But he is a total badass.

Over time, more gods joined the Olympians. Zeus and Hera had two sons: Ares, the violent god of war, and Hephaestus, the gods' blacksmith who was cast off Olympus because he was lame.

Remember Ouranos' genitals? Well, they begot the breathtakingly beautiful Aphrodite, who rose from the ocean to everyone's surprise, presumably. The goddess of love, beauty and sex, Aphrodite was married to Hephaestus but struggled to remain faithful.

Zeus got around. One of his dalliances, with the Titan Leto, produced twins: Apollo and Artemis. Apollo is a truly divine polymath, being the god of the sun, prophecy, poetry, music, medicine, plague and more! Wild child Artemis is the goddess of the moon, archery and hunting. Another of Zeus' flings produced Hermes. As the gods' messenger, Hermes flits between the mortal and divine realms using his iconic winged sandals.

Finally, there's Athena, the goddess of wisdom. To summarize, Zeus had a mighty headache and asked Hephaestus to take an axe to his head; out burst a fully formed Athena. And you thought your migraines were bad.

PANDORA'S JAR

The Titan Prometheus decided that the humans needed fire. In the dead of night, Prometheus sneaked into Hephaestus' forge and stole a burning torch as a gift for the humans.

Zeus was livid. Fire was a powerful tool which brought the humans that bit closer to the gods. Something had to be done. Poor Prometheus was sent to Hades where an eagle would peck out his liver every day for eternity. But the humans had to be punished too, so Zeus sent them a woman.

Her name was Pandora, and she was quite something. The gods had bestowed gifts on her like fairies at Sleeping Beauty's christening: beauty from Aphrodite, talent from Athena and curiosity from Hermes. And Pandora brought with her a jar.

Pandora had been warned never to open her jar, but her curiosity got the better of her, so she popped the lid open. Out poured pain, violence, death, starvation and a hundred other terrible monsters. Only hope, a tiny creature, remained.

The Golden Age of humanity was over.

THE LABOURS OF HERACLES

Humanity needed heroes. And who better than the man who put the "glad" in "gladiator"? Heracles (Hercules to the Romans) was yet another offspring of Zeus, this time with a mortal woman called Alcmene. Hera was furious at Zeus' infidelity, and, in a typical *Hera* move, attempted to plague Heracles with misery for the rest of his life.

Heracles had built up a stunning heroic reputation for himself, but Hera's plan would change that. She drove Heracles into such a ferocious madness that he killed his wife and children. Heracles was horrified by what he'd done and, to atone, pledged servitude to the king Eurystheus. Eurystheus set him ten seemingly impossible tasks: the Labours of Heracles.

Over the following years, Heracles slayed fearsome beasts like the hydra and Nemean lion, and went on numerous fetch quests for Artemis' golden hind, the girdle of Hippolyta and the mares of Diomedes. Heracles even completed two bonus tasks, culminating in the capture of Cerberus, the underworld's three-headed guard dog.

And, to this day, any task that seems insurmountable is called "Herculean".

THESEUS AND THE MINOTAUR

Every year, Athens was forced to send 14 young "tributes" to Crete to suffer a terrible fate. They were sent into the Labyrinth, built by master craftsman Daedalus, where they were devoured by the monstrous Minotaur, offspring of the Cretan Queen Pasiphaë and a bull.

The Athenian prince Theseus had had enough. Shouting "I volunteer as tribute!" (probably) he took the place of one of the youths, and sailed to Crete to slay the Minotaur. Theseus was a total dreamboy, and soon caught the eye of Cretan Princess Ariadne, who sneaked into his prison cell that night for a quick snog and to offer her help. She gave him a ball of thread for navigating the treacherous Labyrinth, and they pledged their love.

The next morning, Theseus entered the Labyrinth, tied his thread to the door, and raced toward the Minotaur. After a tremendous struggle, the beast was dead, and Theseus followed the thread back out of the maze. He and Ariadne escaped from Crete, and Theseus had cemented his reputation as a mighty hero.

THE TROJAN WAR

The epic Trojan War has captured imaginations for thousands of years. And it all began with a beauty pageant. Ordered to choose the most beautiful of Hera, Athena and Aphrodite, Trojan Prince Paris picked Aphrodite because in exchange she'd promised him Helen, the most beautiful woman alive. But when Paris claimed his prize, Helen's existing husband Menelaus got a bit cross and amassed a mighty Greek army to attack Troy.

The resulting war lasted for ten long years, with heroes on both sides seeking glory. Chief among the Greeks was the semi-divine Achilles (dodgy heel and all), ruthless Agamemnon, "the brains" Odysseus and "the brawn" Ajax. The Trojans had hottie Prince Hector, practically perfect in every way, as well as Paris, a whole host of their brothers, and cousin Aeneas (remember him for later).

Eventually, it was cunning Odysseus who ended it all, devising a clever plan to hide Greek soldiers inside a giant wooden horse, and destroy Troy from the inside. Troy was razed to the ground, and the war was over.

HOMER'S *ILIAD*

One of the earliest works of Western literature is the
Iliad, an epic poem about the Trojan War, by Homer.
Although he is referred to as the father of Western
literature, little is known about Homer for sure. Was he
a man, a woman or multiple people? Was he blind? Did
he love Duff Beer and doughnuts? We don't know!

The *Iliad* was originally recounted orally, sung by
bards and poets across the years, before eventually
being written down in around the eighth century BCE.
The poem narrates a period of a few weeks toward the
end of the war, during which Achilles quarrelled with
Agamemnon over a girl (times don't change much, do
they?), threw a major tantrum and refused to continue
fighting. The resulting events culminated in the deaths
of both Patroclus, Achilles' close companion and
probable lover, and Hector, the heir to the Trojan
throne. This set in motion the events that would bring
the war to its bloodthirsty conclusion.

HOMER'S *ODYSSEY*

The sister poem to the *Iliad* is Homer's *Odyssey*. The narrative focuses on the Greek hero Odysseus' ten-year-long journey home after the Trojan War. Although apparently desperate to be reunited with his wife Penelope and son Telemachus, Odysseus was a fan of a side quest, and the poem narrates his run-ins with the cyclops Polyphemus, the witch Circe, the nymph Calypso, the sea monsters Scylla and Charybdis and the alluring Sirens. Along the way, Odysseus lost every single one of his 600 or so crewmates. Every. Single. One.

Eventually, Odysseus made it home to Ithaca, where he killed all 108 of the suitors who, believing him dead, were vying for Penelope's hand. What an ending.

The *Odyssey*, along with the *Iliad*, has had an enormous impact on Western literature and art. The word "odyssey" is still used to describe a lengthy voyage, as fans of *Super Mario Odyssey* will be well aware, and every episodic adventure series or road trip film owes its origins, in some small way, to Odysseus and his terrible navigation skills.

ROMAN MYTHOLOGY

The civilization of ancient Rome lasted from the eighth century BCE to the fifth century CE, but it is the era of the Roman Empire (27 BCE–476 CE) that is probably best known, conjuring up images of knobbly-kneed soldiers, and men in togas saying "carpe diem".

Roman mythology has a lot in common with Greek. The Romans noticed the similarities between the Greek gods and their own and combined them into one, which is why many of these gods are known by two different names. Elsewhere, Greek stories are repurposed with a Roman twist.

The Romans were proud, patriotic people. Their most prominent myths are two accounts of the founding of Rome, myths which gave the Roman people divine lineage and offered justification for the ruling imperial family and continued expansion of the empire.

But the Romans were lovers as well as fighters. Contrary to the common depiction of the Romans as stiff and emotionless, many tales from Roman mythology narrate the joys and sorrows of love.

WHAT'S IN A NAME?

The Romans merged a bunch of the Greek gods with their own existing gods. Use this handy conversion chart to figure out which god the Romans are referring to.

GREEK NAME	ROMAN NAME
Zeus	Jupiter
Hera	Juno
Poseidon	Neptune
Hades	Pluto
Demeter	Ceres
Hestia	Vesta
Hephaestus	Vulcan
Ares	Mars

GREEK NAME	ROMAN NAME
Aphrodite	Venus
Athena	Minerva
Apollo	Apollo (so good they named him once)
Artemis	Diana
Hermes	Mercury
Dionysus (god of wine and partying)	Bacchus
Eros (Aphrodite's son; god of love)	Cupid

VIRGIL'S *AENEID*

Virgil (70-19 BCE) was a Roman poet and major Homer fanboy. He was commissioned by the first Roman Emperor, Augustus, to write an epic poem commemorating the founding of Rome by the Trojan hero Aeneas.

The first half of the *Aeneid* charts Aeneas' voyage to Italy. He and a smattering of Trojans had escaped Troy's destruction and, now refugees, landed at Carthage, a city run by Queen Dido. It wasn't long before Aeneas and Dido fell head over heels in love, but Aeneas was reminded of his destiny to found Rome, and knew he had to leave. Heartbroken, Dido committed suicide as she watched Aeneas' ship fade into the distance.

After a brief interlude in the underworld, Aeneas finally arrived in Italy. In the epic's second half, the Trojans fought for Latium, the region where Rome would eventually be built. Guess what? They were successful, and Aeneas even got a sweet new bride out of the deal, the Latin princess Lavinia. These Trojans would go on to become the first people of Rome.

ROMULUS AND REMUS

So we have the *people* of Rome, but the city itself has its own foundation myth. The story starts in Alba Longa, a city founded by Aeneas' son Ascanius. This is where the twins Romulus and Remus were born, the sons of the god Mars and Rhea Silvia, daughter of the deposed king Numitor.

New king Amulius, Numitor's brother, felt threatened by these potential throne-usurping babies, and ordered them to be drowned in the River Tiber. However, the babies floated merrily down to the site of future Rome and were found by a she-wolf. This wolf suckled the boys until they were discovered and subsequently raised by a shepherd called Faustulus.

When the twins were fully grown, they set out to found their own city. When they couldn't agree where to build it, hostility grew between the brothers to such an extent that, in the end, Romulus murdered Remus. Well, that's one way to get your own way.

Romulus built his city and named it after himself: Rome.

OVID'S *METAMORPHOSES*

The *Metamorphoses* is a poem by Virgil's contemporary, Ovid. In a delicious blend of myth and history, Ovid narrates a range of stories from the beginning of time right up to the deification of Julius Caesar, who was assassinated the year before Ovid was born. As the title would suggest, these stories nearly always involve something being transformed into something else.

One example is the story of Arachne. She was a talented weaver who was confident (or foolish) enough to challenge Minerva, goddess of handicrafts, to a contest. Minerva wove a magnificent tapestry showing scenes of gods punishing mortals for their arrogance. But Arachne's tapestry, which depicted various gods' crimes against humans, was something else entirely. Minerva flew into a jealous rage, tearing up Arachne's work and beating the girl with her spindle. Arachne was so ashamed that she hanged herself.

Minerva took pity on the girl and transformed her into a spider (hence arachnid), hanging from a thread instead of a noose, weaving her silky webs for eternity.

CUPID AND PSYCHE

This story appears in the Roman novel *The Golden Ass* (grow up – it's referring to a donkey).

The young Psyche was so beautiful that Venus went mad with jealousy. She sent her son Cupid to shoot Psyche with his arrow, so that she'd fall in love with someone horrible. But Cupid fell in love with Psyche himself. He married her and whisked her away to his palace.

Psyche's new husband only came to her at night, so that his true identity would be kept secret from her. But she *had* to have a glimpse. So, one night, she lit a candle and gazed upon her beautiful, sleeping husband. Cupid woke and was so furious that he left Psyche and flew away.

Psyche searched endlessly for Cupid. In her wanderings she completed four fiendish tasks set by Venus, who despised her daughter-in-law. Eventually, Jupiter told Venus to back off, granted Psyche immortality and threw a wedding banquet. Cupid and Psyche lived together in eternal bliss.

It's nice to have a happy ending for once.

NORTHERN EUROPE

We're now heading north from Greece and Rome, to the Norse people of Scandinavia and the Celts of the British Isles.

The Norse people, or Norsemen, inhabited Scandinavia during the Early Middle Ages. This era came to be known as the Viking Age, thanks to the Norse seafarers (aka Vikings) who invaded and raided parts of Europe in their distinctive longships between the eighth and eleventh centuries CE. The Norse people enjoyed storytelling, music and drinking, so you'd probably have a good time with them down the pub.

Norse mythology and culture have fired the imaginations of writers and creators throughout the centuries. Richard Wagner's four-part opera series *Der Ring des Nibelungen* (The Ring of the Nibelung) borrowed heavily from Norse myths, and gave us the stereotypical image of horned-helmeted Vikings (devastatingly, there's no evidence that Vikings wore horned helmets). More recent endeavours such as the Marvel superhero Thor, the drama series *Vikings* and a healthy dose of Viking-inspired video games prove that these stories still captivate us today.

The Celtic peoples of Iron Age Britain have a strong legacy in the UK and Ireland – the Welsh, Cornish, Scottish Gaelic and Irish languages, which are descended from the original Celtic language, are all still spoken today. It's thought that Celtic culture originated in Central Europe as early as 1200 BCE, before spreading throughout Western Europe and reaching the British Isles.

The Romans began their (second attempt at) conquest of Britain in 43 CE, but the Celts were willing to put up a fight – Boudicca of the Iceni tribe is a well-known example, and Hadrian's Wall, which in its prime spanned the entire width of the country, was built to keep the Scottish Celts at bay. True to form, the Romans identified many Celtic deities as gods from their own pantheon.

Today, the Celtic peoples are known for their stories and folklore, and the intricate, intertwining patterns of Celtic art. Many mythical creatures and characters from fairy tales have their origin in Celtic myth and folklore, such as fairies themselves, mermaids, pixies and leprechauns.

⤳ NORSE MYTHOLOGY ⤳

Norse mythology developed out of the Old Norse Religion (or Norse Paganism). It was traditionally passed down orally, and most sources we have weren't written down until after the Christianization of Scandinavia between the eighth and twelfth centuries. That means we can't be sure of their authenticity, especially as they do show some evidence of Christian alterations. But they're the best we have!

The two most detailed of these sources are the *Prose Edda* and the *Poetic Edda*. The *Prose Edda* was written in the early thirteenth century by the delightfully named Icelandic poet Snorri Sturluson, and the *Poetic Edda* is a collection of poems with unknown title, author or date. Together, they tell of the creation (and eventual destruction) of the world and the exploits of the gods.

Featured here are well-known Norse celebs Thor, Odin and Loki as well as plenty more colourful characters. Along the way, Thor will become a blushing bride, Loki a questionable hairdresser, and there will be an unfortunate mistletoe-related incident. Relatable stuff.

THE NINE REALMS

It began with the giant Ymir. He had a son, Buri, who in turn had a son called Bor. Bor married the giantess Bestla, and the couple had three robust sons: Ve, Vili and Odin.

Odin and his brothers didn't like Ymir much. They slayed him and built the universe from his corpse. The lands were created from Ymir's flesh, the oceans from his blood, the hills from his bones and the trees from his hair. Ymir's colossal domed skull became the sky. The gods created a fertile realm, Midgard (aka Earth), from Ymir's eyebrows. To inhabit this realm, they created the first man and woman, Ask and Embla, from two fallen trees.

The gods split into two groups: the Aesir, the sky gods who lived in Asgard (reachable via the rainbow bridge Bifröst), and the Vanir, the earth gods who lived in Vanaheim (not Anaheim). Asgard, Vanaheim and Midgard were three of the nine realms connected by the great World Tree, Yggdrasil. Odin took the throne of Asgard, presiding over all nine realms.

THE NORSE PANTHEON

So we've met Odin. He's the one-eyed, staff-wielding king of the Aesir, and through his Germanic name Wodan he gives us Wednesday. He is married to Frigg, or Frigga, who lends her name to Friday.

Odin's most famous son is Thor. This red headed and bearded god of thunder wields the mighty hammer Mjölnir and gives Thursday its name. Thor was popular among the Norsemen and remains popular today, thanks in part to some well-known comics and films.

Odin and Frigg's sons include Baldr, the most beautiful and well loved of the gods, Tyr, the god of war who gives us Tuesday, and Heimdall, the gods' watchman who can see and hear all.

The Vanir are led by Freyr and Freyja, a confusingly named, brother and sister, husband and wife, sky-father and earth-mother couple.

And then there's Loki. No one quite seems to know how he fits in, which is appropriate, since he's a shape-shifting trickster god. Some sources place him as a giant or as Odin's foster brother. You just can't pin this guy down.

A HAIRY SITUATION

One morning, Thor's wife Sif was horrified to discover that her shining golden hair had vanished. Turns out Loki had shaved Sif's head as a prank, but he promised to fix everything.

Loki asked the dwarf sons of Ivaldi to make three treasures for the gods, including a cap of golden hair. But two other dwarves, Brock and Eitri, wagered that they could do better. Loki scoffed and said that if they won, they could chop off his head.

The time came for the dwarves to present their gifts. For Sif, the sons of Ivaldi had crafted a cap of gleaming golden hair. For Odin: a spear which would never miss its mark. And for Freyr: a huge ship that could be folded up and pocketed.

Then it was Brock and Eitri's turn. For Freyr: a golden boar to pull his chariot. For Odin: a gold ring that multiplied every night. And for Thor: the mighty hammer Mjölnir. Everyone was psyched, and declared Brock and Eitri the winners. Loki even wriggled out of his decapitation on a technicality. Smiles all round!

THE WEDDING OF THOR

"Where's Mjölnir?" roared Thor. His beloved hammer had vanished, so he enlisted the help of Loki to find it. Loki eventually located Mjölnir in the house of the giant Thrym. But there was a catch: Thrym would only return Mjölnir in exchange for Freyja's hand in marriage.

"Absolutely no way," said Freyja, so Heimdall came up with a cunning plan. They would dress Thor as a bride, with a beautiful gown and thick veil. Thrym wasn't the sharpest. He probably wouldn't notice the difference.

At the wedding feast, Thor (aka Mrs Thrym) ate and ate and ate. Thrym frowned. He'd never known a woman with such an appetite. Her bridesmaid (Loki) reassured Thrym that "Freyja" was so excited about the wedding that she hadn't eaten for days. Thrym reckoned that made sense.

Thrym ordered that Mjölnir be placed on his bride's lap to bless the marriage. Thor seized his hammer, tore off his veil and went full bridezilla, killing Thrym and all the other giants. Gotta love a wedding.

BRYNHILDR AND SIGURD

Brynhildr was a Valkyrie, one of a band of female Asgardian warriors. She had displeased Odin and was condemned to eternal sleep surrounded by a ring of fire.

But don't worry! The noble hero Sigurd rode to Brynhildr's rescue, diving through the flames and waking her with a kiss. He promised to marry her. But before he got the chance, Sigurd was poisoned with a potion that made him forget poor Brynhildr. Instead, he married a princess called Gudrun.

Gudrun's brother Gunnar fancied Brynhildr for himself, but was too cowardly to jump through the ring of fire. Sigurd took pity on Gunnar, so assumed Gunnar's form and leaped through the flames. Brynhildr and "Gunnar" got married. Afterwards, Sigurd reassumed his own form and switched places with the real Gunnar.

Gudrun eventually revealed to Brynhildr that it had been Sigurd who had rescued her. Brynhildr felt betrayed and humiliated, and convinced Gunnar to murder Sigurd. But upon seeing Sigurd dead, Brynhildr was so overcome with grief and love that she threw herself onto his funeral pyre, dying alongside him.

BALDR

Odin and Frigg's son Baldr was the most beloved of all the gods. Everyone loved him. Except (drum roll please) Loki! He vowed to find Baldr's weakness.

But Baldr was practically invincible, because Frigg had made every single object swear never to hurt her son. The other gods, knowing Baldr was immune to harm, entertained themselves by using him as target practice.

But Loki tricked Frigg into revealing Baldr's one weakness: mistletoe. Laughing to himself, Loki fashioned a dart from a mistletoe plant and handed it to Hodr, Baldr's blind brother. The unsuspecting Hodr, wanting to join in the game, hurled it at his brother. Baldr dropped dead.

Devastated, Frigg sent her son Hermod to the underworld (Hel) to convince its ruling goddess (also Hel) to resurrect Baldr. Hel agreed, but only if everyone alive wept for him. Baldr was so beloved that everyone *did* weep, all except for one giantess, Thökk.

And so Baldr spent eternity in Hel. Or did he?

RAGNARÖK

Ragnarök is the Norse apocalypse: the death of the Aesir and the destruction of the world. And the best part? It hasn't happened yet, so we have all this to look forward to, folks.

The first sign that Ragnarök approaches will be three years of back-to-back winters. This will bring bitter hardship, and soon we'll all be so hangry that we start killing each other: father against son, sister against sister, friend against friend.

Three roosters will crow, waking the giants, the gods and the dead in Hel. The World Tree Yggdrasil will shudder and writhe. The giant wolf Fenrir will break free from his chains, devouring everything in his path. The gods will fight the forces of destruction, but they are doomed to die, and the world will be consumed by the oceans.

But all is not lost. Some say a new world will rise from the sea, and will be ruled by the few surviving gods, including our old friend Baldr.

It's just a shame we'll all be dead by then.

∽⊙ CELTIC MYTHOLOGY ⊙∽

Celtic mythology stemmed from the Ancient Celtic religion (sometimes called Celtic paganism), and is rich with gods and kings, creatures and beings, and one very special salmon.

Celtic mythology features a number of subgroups which are mostly distinct, although some elements are shared between them. The god Lugh, for example, appears throughout many different Celtic mythologies. Some of these subgroups are Irish, Scottish, Welsh and Cornish mythology.

Many of the stories featured here originate from the comparatively well-attested Irish mythology. The surviving writings have been divided into four collections, or cycles: the Mythological Cycle, which recounts tales of the pantheon called the Tuatha Dé Danann, the Ulster Cycle, which features heroes such as Cú Chulainn, the Fenian Cycle, which stars the hero Fionn mac Cumhaill and his warriors the Fianna, and the Historical Cycle, which narrates stories of the legendary kings of Ireland.

And there's also a hapless Welsh prince here for good measure.

THE TUATHA DÉ DANANN

One Irish pantheon is the Tuatha Dé Danann, a supernatural race often thought to represent gods. Key members include the fatherlike Dagda, the queen of doom Morrigan, the god of war Lugh, and the goddess of wisdom and healing Brigid. And they were all really good at getting into fights.

Round 1: The first battle of Mag Tuired. The Tuatha Dé Danann invaded the land of Ireland, overthrew the Fir Bolg people who lived there, and settled themselves as Ireland's rulers.

Round 2: The second battle of Mag Tuired. The Tuatha Dé Danann fought to free themselves from the oppression of their monstrous rivals, the Fomorians.

Round 3: The battle with the Milesians. The Tuatha Dé Danann battled with new invaders, the Milesians from Iberia. Eventually, an agreement was reached: the Milesians would occupy the land above ground, and the Tuatha Dé Danann would live in the Otherworld, the realm of the gods and the dead.

And so the Milesians became the Irish people.

THE DAGDA'S HARP

The Dagda owned a beautiful harp. It produced music so divine that it could influence emotions and even change the seasons. During the Tuatha Dé Danann's battle with the Fomorians, the Dagda's harp roused the warriors and brought relief to the wounded. The Fomorians found this pretty annoying, so while the Dagda was out fighting they snuck into his house and stole the harp.

The thieves fled to an abandoned castle, where they remained until the Fomorians were defeated and the Dagda realized his harp was missing. He marched to the castle and saw his beloved harp displayed on the wall. He held out his hand, and the harp flew across the room toward him.

But the commotion had woken the thieves, who seized their weapons. Quickly, the Dagda played three songs: one of joy, which made the men drop their weapons and laugh, one of sorrow, which made them weep uncontrollably, and one of sleep, which made them collapse into a deep slumber.

And so the Dagda won back his harp.

CELTIC CREATURES

The different Celtic mythologies have given us a whole host of mythical creatures and beings. Here's an introduction to just a few.

LEPRECHAUN	These little, bearded, mischievous folk originated in Irish mythology, but didn't become prominent until later folklore.
PIXIE	Another type of small, childish, mischievous being, pixies are associated with Cornish mythology.
CHANGELING	A changeling is a type of fairy left in place of a human child that has been stolen by fairies.
MERMAID	Mermaids of British myth and folklore often brought bad luck and disaster, luring men to their deaths.
KELPIE	Kelpies are Scottish water spirits that can shape-shift between a horse and a woman. Some think the Loch Ness Monster is a kelpie!
SELKIE	Another water-based shape-shifter, a selkie can change from a seal to a human by shedding its skin.
BANSHEE	From Irish folklore, this terrifying female spirit signals an approaching death by... screaming her head off.
DULLAHAN	The Irish Dullahan is a headless horseman who rides a black horse. Whenever he comes to a stop, someone is going to die.

THE CHILDREN OF LIR

This tragic tale is thought to have inspired the ballet *Swan Lake*.

Lir and Aoibh lived with their daughter and three sons. When Aoibh tragically passed away, Lir married Aoibh's sister Aoife, and for a while things seemed good. But Aoife was jealous of her dead sister's children. She took them to a lake in order to kill them, but she couldn't bring herself to do the deed, so instead she transformed them into four white swans. The spell would last for 900 years, but the children retained their voices.

When his children didn't return, a panicked Lir travelled to the lake. There, he discovered the four swans, who told him about Aoife's treachery. There was nothing Lir could do except wait by the lake, listening to his children's mournful singing.

At long last, 900 years passed. Lir was long dead. A mist enveloped the swans and they were transformed into humans once more. But time had taken its toll. The children became ancient and withered, and they perished.

CÚ CHULAINN

Cú Chulainn, hero of Ulster, was the son and incarnation of the war god Lugh. One day, Ulster came under attack from Queen Mebh of Connaught. Disastrously, Ulster's warriors had all been cursed to suffer debilitating labour pains (sucks, doesn't it, boys?). All, that was, except Cú Chulainn.

So, at the ripe old age of 17, Cú Chulainn faced the Connaughtmen alone. He battled courageously, but after one bout of fighting he was badly injured. As he recuperated in bed, the Ulster youth corps fought in his place, and were slaughtered. Luckily, Cú Chulainn had this neat trick called ríastrad (one translation is "warp-spasm"...) which turned him into a destructive monster. He avenged the youth corps.

The climax of the war was the battle between Cú Chulainn and his friend Ferdiad. Cú Chulainn begged his friend to withdraw, but Ferdiad refused, so Cú Chulainn was forced to fight and kill him. Eventually, the Ulstermen recovered and, led by Cú Chulainn, defeated the Connaughtmen. Do not mess with this guy.

THE SALMON OF KNOWLEDGE

This exquisitely titled tale stars the warrior hero Fionn mac Cumhaill, whose name is often rendered, wait for it, Finn McCool.

When Fionn was but a young lad, he went to stay with the poet Finegas. Finegas had spent seven years fishing for the salmon of knowledge, which would grant all-worldly knowledge to whomever was first to taste its flesh. Soon after Fionn arrived, Finegas at last caught the salmon.

Finegas asked Fionn to cook the salmon, instructing him not to eat even a single mouthful. Fionn obeyed, but, as he was turning the fish over, he burned his thumb and instinctively started sucking it. A single drop of salmon fat had been on his thumb and all the salmon's knowledge was now coursing through his veins. There was nothing Finegas could do except let the boy eat the rest.

From then on, Fionn could call on the salmon's wisdom simply by sucking his thumb, and this power helped him become the leader of the mighty Fianna. Now that's McCool.

PWYLL AND RHIANNON

Prince Pwyll hails from Welsh mythology, if you didn't already guess from the absence of vowels in his name.

Pwyll was having a great day. An amazingly beautiful woman, Rhiannon, had asked to marry him. There was only one hitch: she was already engaged to an odious man called Gwawl. But they got married anyway.

At the wedding feast, some guy asked Pwyll for one favour. Pwyll, in a questionable move, said, "Sure, whatever you want," at which point the guy revealed himself to be Gwawl and demanded Rhiannon. Pwyll had no choice but to agree.

Rhiannon was *so* mad, but she hatched a plan. At her and Gwawl's wedding feast, Pwyll asked Gwawl to fill his bag with food. But, however much food was put into the bag, it was never full. Pwyll explained that the bag could only be filled if a nobleman stepped inside. Gwawl jumped straight into the bag, and Rhiannon and Pwyll trapped him inside – of course.

SOUTH AND EAST ASIA

Hindu mythology of the Indian religion Hinduism, Chinese mythology from Ancient and Imperial China, and Japanese mythology from the Shinto and Buddhist traditions are a trio as diverse as they are exciting.

Hinduism originates from the Indian subcontinent and is a *dharma* (a way of life, a system of morality) as much as a religion. It has no single founder, but is a collection or synthesis of many different beliefs and practices. Hindu gods such as the four-armed Vishnu or the blue-skinned Krishna will be familiar, as will Hindu beliefs and concepts like karma, the principle of cause and effect.

The earliest dynasty of Ancient China is thought to be the Xia dynasty of approximately 2070–1600 BCE, who lived in the Yellow River valley. Following them was the Shang dynasty (around 1600–1046 BCE), who produced the oldest surviving Chinese written records: inscribed oracle bones. Imperial China began in 221 BCE when Qin Shi Huang unified China and declared himself emperor, and successive dynasties kept the Imperial system going until 1912.

Chinese culture is one of the oldest in the world, and is distinctive and influential in countless areas, including arts, ceramics, architecture, cuisine, martial arts, music, theatre and philosophy. Chinese festivals and traditions are also recognizable the world over – think fireworks, lanterns and dancing dragons.

Japan's kingdoms and tribes were unified over the course of several hundred years between the fourth and ninth centuries CE. But traditionally, Japan's first emperor is much older than that: the legendary Emperor Jimmu is said to have ruled from 660 BCE. One hundred and twenty-five emperors later, the Imperial House of Japan is still going strong today.

Japanese culture has had a profound impact on the Western world. The kimono, samurai, sumo wrestling and ninjas are all aspects of Japanese culture that are instantly recognizable. We also have the Land of the Rising Sun to thank for sushi, origami, anime, Pokémon and all things *kawaii* like Hello Kitty. The mythology of Japan is just one aspect of the country's vibrant culture and legacy.

⤳ HINDU MYTHOLOGY ⤳

Hinduism is the oldest still-practised religion in the world, with some traditions dating back as far as 2000 BCE or even earlier. Today, Hinduism has over 1.2 billion followers, with a range of different beliefs, philosophies, traditions, practices and rituals. The body of mythology is correspondingly huge, and includes numerous texts such as the Vedas, Puranas, and the epics *Mahabharata* and *Ramayana*, all of which are written in Sanskrit, the sacred language of Hinduism. What's provided here is only a snapshot.

With such a long and varied history that continues to this day, it's no surprise that these myths are often more fluid than they seem to be in other traditions, with much regional and temporal variation. Gods will change names and even functions depending on when and where you are. This complex web can seem confusing if you're unfamiliar with this mythology, but these stories and characters are vibrant and exciting, telling rich tales of gods and heroes, love and war. So it's well worth just diving in head first.

THE TRIMURTI

To many, the deities in Hinduism are considered different aspects of Brahman. Brahman is the spiritual core of the universe; not so much a god but the essence of reality itself. Brahman is also personified as three gods: the Trimurti.

Brahma (without the "n") is the creator. He's often depicted as red-skinned, with four arms and four heads. He was responsible for the creation of the universe.

Vishnu is the preserver. He protects all life in the universe, often taking different incarnations called avatars. His ten main avatars are called the Dashavatara, and include Matsya the fish, Narasimha the man-lion, Krishna and Rama (both of whom we'll meet shortly), and the Buddha.

Shiva is the destroyer. His role, as the name suggests, is to destroy the universe. But don't panic: this is all so that the universe can be reborn and improved upon. Shiva is also the god of yoga, so give him a thank you next time you're doing the downward dog.

GODS OF HINDU MYTHOLOGY

Here is a starter pack of Hindu gods and goddesses to get you going. There are many, many more.

INDRA	Indra is the king of the gods and heaven, and god of thunder, storms, rain and war.
MAHADEVI	Also called Devi or Shakti, Mahadevi is the supreme mother goddess. Some believe she manifests as the goddesses Saraswati, Lakshmi and Parvati.
GANESHA	This many-armed, elephant-headed god is a patron of wisdom and intellect, the arts and sciences, and new beginnings.
SARASWATI	Knowledge, music, art and learning are Saraswati's domains. She is the wife of Brahma.
LAKSHMI	Lakshmi is the goddess of fortune, fertility and prosperity, and the consort of Vishnu.
PARVATI	Parvati is patron of love, beauty and marriage. She is married to Shiva. She, Saraswati and Lakshmi (the wives of Brahma and Vishnu) form the trinity of Hindu goddesses called the Tridevi.

THE BIRTH OF KRISHNA

The Puranas are a huge genre of Indian literature, telling tales of the gods and heroes. One famous Purana is the Bhagavata Purana, which features tales of the birth and childhood of Krishna, one of Vishnu's avatars.

Krishna's parents were Vasudeva and Devaki, from the city Mathura. Devaki was the sister of Mathura's king, Kamsa, a paranoid tyrant who had heard a prophecy that he would be killed by Devaki's child. So, he unceremoniously threw his sister and brother-in-law into prison.

There, Vasudeva and Devaki produced a number of children (prison is boring y'all), but all were murdered by Kamsa. Upon the birth of their eighth child, however, Vasudeva and Devaki were surprised to discover the doors of their cell miraculously open. Guided by a divine voice, Vasudeva smuggled his newborn son out of Mathura and across the Yamuna River to his friend Nanda.

Nanda and his wife Yashoda raised the baby as their own, so that Kamsa would never find him. This child grew up to become Krishna.

THE *MAHABHARATA*

One of two Sanskrit epics central to Hindu mythology, the *Mahabharata* is the longest epic poem ever written, being approximately ten times longer than Homer's *Iliad* and *Odyssey* combined. So, summarizing it is no easy feat. But here goes.

The epic narrates the struggle for the throne of Hastinapur between two sets of cousins: the Kaurava princes and the Pandava princes. The Kauravas were the more senior branch of the family, but the oldest Pandava was older than the oldest Kaurava. So, war it was.

In one episode, the Kauravas built the Pandavas a palace, then set it alight. But the Pandavas escaped through a secret tunnel. Later, Duryodhana and Yudhishthira, the oldest Kaurava and Pandava respectively, competed in a dice game. But the dice were loaded in Duryodhana's favour, and Yudhishthira lost all his wealth and his kingdom. The Pandavas were exiled for 13 years, then returned to fight the Kurukshetra War, eventually emerging victorious.

The epic's narrative is broken up by philosophical discourses and other tales. Such as...

SHAKUNTALA

Shakuntala's new husband Dushyanta, king of Hastinapur, was so gorgeous that she spent all her time daydreaming about him. When the sage Durvasa visited her, the distracted Shakuntala neglected to offer him hospitality. Durvasa was furious and cursed her, saying that whomever she was dreaming of would forget all about her.

But when Durvasa learned that Shakuntala was simply in love, he softened the curse, so that Dushyanta would remember Shakuntala if shown a token of their love. Shakuntala looked at the royal ring Dushyanta had given her. Surely that would do the trick? She set out to find him at his royal court.

On the way to Dushyanta, Shakuntala accidentally dropped her ring in a river. When she arrived at court, her beloved Dushyanta did not recognize her. Heartbroken, she fled to the forest.

Meanwhile, a fisherman was understandably surprised to find a royal ring in the belly of a fish. He took it to Dushyanta, who immediately remembered Shakuntala. The curse was broken. Dushyanta rushed to the forest, and husband and wife were reunited.

THE *RAMAYANA*

The *Ramayana*, the other major Sanskrit epic, tells the story of Prince Rama, another avatar of Vishnu.

Rama was heir to the throne of Ayodhya, but due to a succession argument (it's always the way, isn't it?) he was exiled, along with his wife Sita and brother Lakshmana. In exile, Sita was kidnapped by the demon Ravana, who was hell-bent on destroying Rama. Ravana proposed marriage to Sita, but she refused, remaining loyal to Rama.

Meanwhile, the monkey god Hanuman offered to help Rama search for Sita. He eventually found her being harassed by Ravana and his companions. Hanuman showed Sita Rama's ring and offered to take her away. Great! But Sita refused, saying that it was only proper that Rama be the one to rescue her.

Rama, Lakshmana and Hanuman prepared for battle with Ravana. After a mighty war, Rama defeated Ravana, and was reunited with Sita. They returned to Ayodhya, where Rama took his rightful place on the throne. This homecoming is celebrated at the festival of Diwali.

DURGA

The buffalo demon Mahishasura went about the place like he was invincible. He tortured innocent people and waged war against the gods. For it was said that Mahishasura could only be killed by a woman. Which made him immortal, right? Because no woman could ever be strong enough to defeat him.

How wrong he was.

The gods were panicked by Mahishasura's behaviour, so the Trimurti combined all their power and created a ruthless warrior goddess. She had many hands, each armed with a deadly weapon. She rode a colossal lion. This was Durga.

The battle between Durga and Mahishasura was violent and confusing. Mahishasura unleashed hundreds of demons, but Durga slayed them all. Mahishasura tried shape-shifting to confuse the goddess – first a lion, then a man, then an elephant – but with a little lassoing here, a little decapitation there, Durga was always one step ahead. Finally, with Mahishasura back in his buffalo form, Durga pierced him with her trident and decapitated him. Again. Do not mess with this goddess.

∽ CHINESE MYTHOLOGY ∼

Chinese mythology and folklore are fundamental aspects of Chinese folk religion, which encompasses a range of traditions and practices of the Han Chinese people (the world's largest ethnic group, totalling about 18 per cent of the world's population). Because of the size of China and its long history, there is a huge range of different characters and themes in the mythology of this region.

Chinese myths are concerned with the creation of the world and the origins of Chinese traditions and customs. Many feature the Jade Emperor, who rules heaven and keeps everything on earth ticking over nicely. These tales have been passed down orally and written down in poems or narratives, such as *Journey to the West*, a novel from the sixteenth century which features the story of Sun Wukong.

In the next pages we have origin stories for a couple of different Chinese festivals as well as the Chinese Zodiac, a serpentine love story and a chaotic and easily distracted monkey king.

PANGU

In the beginning, there was nothing but swirling chaos. This chaos amassed together and formed a giant cosmic egg, inside which the opposing forces of yin and yang battled. Eventually, they found balance and union, and from this union Pangu was formed.

Pangu had two horns and two tusks, and was completely covered in hair. Taking his great axe, Pangu split the egg and emerged. Yin and yang were released, and formed the earth and the sky. Standing between them, Pangu lifted the sky away from the earth, each day growing taller until the sky reached its current position. Exhausted by this task, Pangu lay down and died.

His final breath became the clouds, his spine the mountains, his eyes the sun and moon, his flesh the soil, his bones the rocks and minerals, and his blood the rivers. His limbs became the four pillars that hold up the sky.

The human race evolved from the fleas that roamed Pangu's body. Explains a lot when you think about it.

CHANG'E

The story of the moon goddess Chang'e has many versions. Here's one.

One morning, everyone was surprised to discover that, instead of the usual one, *ten* suns had risen into the sky. This caused widespread destruction and some nasty sunburns, so everyone was pretty mad.

Luckily, the skilled archer Hou Yi was able to shoot down nine of the suns until just one remained. For this heroic act, he was awarded the elixir of immortality, crowned king, and generally lauded as a saviour. But fame went to Hou Yi's head, and he became a power-hungry tyrant. His wife Chang'e knew that if he drank the elixir of immortality, his people would never be free from oppression. So she drank it first.

Now immortal, Chang'e couldn't remain on earth, so she drifted toward the moon. Furious, Hou Yi chased after her, trying to shoot her down, but she evaded him. And the moon is where she remains. At the Mid-Autumn festival, people leave out gifts to thank Chang'e for what she did.

SUN WUKONG THE MONKEY KING

The monkey king Sun Wukong longed to be immortal. First, he learned immortality from a martial artist. Then, he wriggled out of his own death by erasing his name from the Book of Life and Death. The Jade Emperor wasn't thrilled. He decided the best way to control Sun Wukong was to give him a job in heaven. But Sun Wukong thought he was too good for his new job, so he absconded after approximately five seconds.

At this point, Sun Wukong started calling himself "Great Sage Equal to Heaven", which did NOT go down well with the Jade Emperor. He tried, and failed, to arrest Sun Wukong, so made him guard the peaches of immortality instead. Sun Wukong, surprise surprise, ate all the peaches, and a pill of immortality, and an awful lot of wine, so now he was quadruply immortal and drunk. He single-handedly destroyed the entire army of heaven, no sweat.

At last, the Jade Emperor summoned the Buddha, who imprisoned Sun Wukong under a mountain for 500 years. Cheeky monkey.

THE LEGEND OF THE WHITE SNAKE

Bai Suzhen was a white snake who lived in a lake. One day, she transformed herself into a beautiful young woman. She met a young man called Xu Xian on the lake's bridge, just as it started to rain. Xu Xian offered Bai Suzhen his umbrella, sparking a beautiful romance. In time they married.

But the monk Fahai knew that Bai Suzhen was really a snake. He urged Xu Xian to give Bai Suzhen realgar wine, which contained arsenic and would force her to reveal her true identity. Xu Xian loved his wife, but Fahai's words troubled him. He gave the wine to Bai Suzhen. She instantly transformed into a white snake, and Xu Xian dropped dead with shock.

But Bai Suzhen wasn't giving up on her love. She knew of a powerful herb that could revive the dead. She found the herb, returned home and gave it to Xu Xian. He instantly came back to life and embraced Bai Suzhen. Snake or not, she was his wife and he loved her. Couple goals!

CHINESE NEW YEAR

The Nian was a terrifying, man-eating beast, with a lion's head and razor-sharp teeth. Each new year, the Nian tore through a village, destroying everyone and everything in sight.

The villagers weren't giving up easily. Over time they observed that the Nian was scared of three things: fire, loud noises and the colour red. So they formed a plan. On New Year's Eve, the villagers dressed their windows and doors with red decorations, donned red robes and strung red lanterns throughout the village. And they waited.

Soon they heard the Nian's mighty roar. It was now or never. The villagers started making as much noise as they could, with drums and gongs and their own raised voices. They set off firecrackers and fireworks. The village was awash with blazing light and engulfed by a terrible cacophony.

The Nian whimpered, backed off and ran away in fear. The village was saved. And so the traditions of wearing red, lighting lanterns and setting off fireworks at the Chinese New Year were born.

THE CHINESE ZODIAC

Needing a way to divide up time, the Jade Emperor decreed that the first 12 animals to cross his river would be given a spot on the calendar.

Rat was crafty and asked kind-hearted Ox for a lift. But at the finish line, Rat jumped from Ox's head to snipe first place. Ox made do with second, and speedy Tiger took bronze. Rabbit, who'd nimbly hopped across the river's stepping stones, was fourth. Fifth was Dragon, who could've flown into first place easily, but had stopped to help others along the way. It looked like Horse would be sixth, but suddenly Snake appeared, spooking him. Snake slithered into sixth place and Horse was pushed into seventh.

Goat, Monkey and Rooster arrived at the finish line together, having teamed up to build a raft. They placed eighth, ninth and tenth, but the real prize was the friends they made along the way. Eleventh was Dog who, although a strong swimmer, got distracted playing in the water. Finally came Pig, who'd stopped for a snack and a nap on the way (relatable).

Which zodiac animal are you? Find your birth year on the chart opposite.

RAT	2020, 2008, 1996, 1984, 1972	Quick-thinking, resourceful, ambitious. Do not trust.
OX	2021, 2009, 1997, 1985, 1973	Hard-working and dependable. Too trusting.
TIGER	2022, 2010, 1998, 1986, 1974	Competitive. Bit intense.
RABBIT	2011, 1999, 1987, 1975, 1963	Quiet. Too quiet. Keep an eye on them.
DRAGON	2012, 2000, 1988, 1976, 1964	Enthusiastic, generous and kind. Also a DRAGON so that's cool.
SNAKE	2013, 2001, 1989, 1977, 1965	Charming and cunning. C'mon, it's a snake.
HORSE	2014, 2002, 1990, 1978, 1966	Confident and determined. Fitness nut.
GOAT	2015, 2003, 1991, 1979, 1967	Friendly and empathetic. Hates conflict but too quiet to say anything.
MONKEY	2016, 2004, 1992, 1980, 1968	Curious and fun-loving. Here for a good time.
ROOSTER	2017, 2005, 1993, 1981, 1969	Diligent and brave. Annoying in the morning.
DOG	2018, 2006, 1994, 1982, 1970	Kind, loyal, friendly. Good boi.
PIG	2019, 2007, 1995, 1983, 1971	Just wants to chill. Always has snacks.

∽ JAPANESE MYTHOLOGY ∽

Enter a weird and wonderful world of spirits, mysterious creatures, bickering siblings and unconventional love. Japanese mythology has its roots in the Shinto and Buddhist religions. Shinto centres on *kami* (beings somewhere between a god and a spirit) which are thought to live inside all things. *Kami* feature prominently in Japanese myths, especially those concerning the origins of the world (they've been called "gods" in the following pages).

Two important sources for Japanese myths are the *Kojiki* and the *Nihon Shoki*. The *Kojiki* is an account of myths and legends and is thought to have been written in the early eighth century, making it the oldest surviving work of Japanese literature. The *Nihon Shoki* was completed in the year 720 CE and contains a detailed account of Japanese myths and history.

These tales have provided inspiration for Japanese pop culture, including Studio Ghibli films, Nintendo video games, and anime shows like *Sailor Moon*. These stories have had an enduring influence on Japan and places further afield.

KUNIUMI

In the beginning, two generations of gods came into being: first the Kotoamatsukami, followed by the Kamiyonanayo. Among the Kamiyonanayo were Izanagi and Izanami, yet another brother-and-sister, husband-and-wife duo.

But the earth was nothing but a soupy mush. Izanagi and Izanami were tasked with bringing form to the earth with a jewel-encrusted spear. The couple stirred the earth-mush with the spear, and the drops on the spear's tip became the first island, Onogoroshima.

Izanami then remarked that she had an unfinished part between her legs. Izanagi replied that between his legs was an... extra part, and they should see what happened when they joined them together. So they carried out a marriage ritual, did the deed and, predictably, a child was born: Hiruko.

But Hiruko was born without bones, because Izanami, the wife, had spoken first in the marriage ritual. How *dare* she. Hiruko was cast into the sea, and Izanagi and Izanami carried out the marriage ritual *properly* this time, resulting in the birth of the islands of Japan.

KAMIUMI

After Hiruko, Izanami fell pregnant again with the fire god Kagutsuchi. But during the birth, he - being the fire god - burned Izanami's womb and vagina, and she died from her terrible wounds.

Blinded by grief, Izanagi crushed his newborn son in a mad fury. He was determined to get his wife back. He travelled to the land of the dead, Yomi, and there he found Izanami. But it wasn't a pretty sight. She was a rotting corpse, with putrid flesh and entrails hanging off her bones. Izanagi fled, and was chased out of Yomi by the demon Shikome.

Well, that didn't go as planned. Izanagi very much needed a shower.

He carried out a ritual purification, and from the water that poured over him, three gods were born: Amaterasu, goddess of the sun, dripping from Izanagi's right eye; Tsukuyomi, deity of the moon, from his left eye; and Susanoo, god of storms, from his nose. They became known as the three precious children.

AMATERASU IN THE CAVE

Susanoo was a troublemaker. After getting kicked out of heaven, he decided to visit his big sister Amaterasu. But they argued, and Susanoo lost his temper and threw a horse into Amaterasu's weaving hall. Siblings, am I right?

Sick of her brother's antics, Amaterasu stormed off into a cave. This was bad news as, without the sun goddess, the world was deprived of life-giving sunlight. The gods decided to entice Amaterasu out.

Plan A was to lure Amaterasu out with a bunch of noisy roosters. Didn't work. Plan B was to hang a large mirror outside the cave so that Amaterasu would be enticed out by her own reflection. Didn't work.

Plan C involved the goddess of fun and partying, Ame-no-Uzume. She jumped up and started performing an enthusiastic striptease, tearing her clothes off with joyful abandon. Amaterasu heard the commotion and finally emerged from her cave to see... probably more than she had bargained for. The gods quickly sealed off the cave, and sunlight was restored to the world.

THE FIRST EMPEROR JIMMU

Japan's first emperor was a legendary figure called Jimmu. He ruled Japan from 660–585 BCE, until his death aged 125. According to myth, Jimmu was a direct descendant of the sun goddess Amaterasu, giving him and every subsequent emperor a divine lineage.

Amaterasu sent her grandson Ninigi to control all the deities on earth. But Ninigi immediately got distracted by – what else – a beautiful girl. She was Sakuya-hime, and the pair instantly fell in love. Ninigi asked Sakuya-hime's father for permission to marry her, but the father offered his older daughter, Iwa-Naga-hime, instead. Ninigi found Iwa-Naga-hime hideously ugly and rejected her. Because of this, he and his descendants would be cursed with short lives.

Ninigi and Sakuya-hime had three sons together: Hoderi, Hosuseri and Hoori. Hoori married Toyotama-hime (who turned out to be a dragon, as you do) and their son, Ugayafukiaezu, was Emperor Jimmu's father.

The red circle on the Japanese flag represents the sun goddess and the legitimacy of her descendants to rule Japan as its emperors.

THE TALE OF PRINCESS KAGUYA

Once, a bamboo cutter was, um, cutting bamboo when he discovered a baby girl inside a bamboo stalk. The bamboo cutter and his wife had no children, so decided to raise this girl as their own, naming her Kaguya.

Rather delightfully, the bamboo cutter now found a gold nugget inside every bamboo stalk he cut. The family became super rich, and Kaguya grew super beautiful. It wasn't long before five noble suitors were tripping over themselves to marry her.

Kaguya didn't fancy marriage, so she asked each suitor to find an elusive treasure, promising she would marry whoever obtained their item first. Three suitors returned with forgeries, the fourth gave up and the fifth died trying. The emperor himself also tried his luck, but Kaguya swiftly friend-zoned him.

Things took a turn when Kaguya revealed that she came from the moon and would have to return there. The emperor sent his guards to protect Kaguya, but a celestial embassy arrived and blinded them all. Kaguya left with the embassy, ascending to her true home, the moon.

MYTHICAL BEINGS

Japanese mythology and folklore have a rich menagerie of beasts and beings.

Yokai are supernatural spirits who can be benevolent, mischievous or malicious. They might look like animals, humans or inanimate objects.

Tsukumogami are household objects that have obtained a spirit. When an object turns 100 years old it becomes a tsukumogami. They're mostly harmless but can develop a vengeful streak if mistreated or discarded.

Shikigami are spirits conjured to carry out their master's dirty work like stealing or spying. They are invisible but can take the form of small paper dolls. Shikigami feature in the animated film *Spirited Away*.

Kitsune, or foxes, are intelligent, shape-shifting creatures in Japanese folklore. They have up to nine tails and are the inspiration for the appropriately named Pokémon Ninetales.

Tanuki, or Japanese raccoon dogs, are mischievous creatures known as bake-danuki when they appear in folklore. They can shape-shift and even possess humans. Everyone's favourite *Animal Crossing* landlord, Tom Nook, is a tanuki and derives his name from the animal.

THE JOROGUMO

Here's a fun little love story about a woodcutter and a murderous spider demon.

The locals knew to avoid the lake, for it was inhabited by a jorogumo – a terrifying spider yokai who could drag men to their watery deaths. But an unsuspecting visiting woodcutter stumbled upon the lake, where he met a beautiful woman. And guess what? They fell in love.

The woodcutter returned to the lake every day to visit his beloved. But the local Buddhist priest knew about this woman's true spidery nature and accompanied the woodcutter one day. He started chanting, and a spiderweb sprang from the water.

The woodcutter now knew his girlfriend was a spider demon. But he wasn't deterred. He sought out permission to marry the jorogumo, but was rejected. He ran back to the lake, was ensnared in spiderwebs and dragged under the water. He was never seen again.

Perhaps the jorogumo and the woodcutter lived out their days in blissful love. Or perhaps she ate him.

SOUTH AND CENTRAL AMERICA

The Mayan, Aztec and Inca civilizations are often mixed up. It's easy to think of Machu Picchu, golden sun discs and human sacrifice, and combine them into one vaguely Mexican, vaguely ancient civilization. But the Maya, Aztec and Inca peoples were from different places and different times, and have correspondingly different cultures to explore. And while their mythologies have some overlap, there are plenty of individual quirks to get stuck into as well.

The Maya peoples are much older and longer lasting than either the Aztecs or the Incas. Situated in what is now south-eastern Mexico, Belize, Guatemala, and western Honduras and El Salvador, Mayan civilization began developing in around 2000 BCE and flourished until the ninth century CE. The great Mayan cities had mostly disappeared before Spanish conquistadors arrived in the sixteenth century to colonize the Meso-American area. Today, the Maya peoples are best remembered for their writing system (the most developed in the pre-Columbian Americas), impressive pyramid-temples, and for *definitely not* predicting the end of the world in 2012.

The Aztec Empire of central Mexico is strikingly recent by comparison. Formed of an alliance of three city states (Tenochtitlan, Tetzcoco and Tlacopan) in 1428, the empire flourished for less than a hundred years before it was conquered by the Spanish in 1521. Mexico City was built on the ruins of Tenochtitlan, and the Aztec people mostly died from famine, forced labour or European diseases. The Aztecs were proficient pyramid builders, skilled in agriculture and partial to human sacrifice. Their language, Nahuatl, gave us such words as avocado, chilli and chocolate. Yum!

The Incas came from further south, occupying the Andes mountains on a large stretch of South America's west coast. Arising in the early thirteenth century, the Inca civilization also didn't have long to wait until the Spanish invaded in 1532. In their heyday, the Incas boasted a magnificent central city, Cuzco, an impressive system for recording information on knotted strings called *quipu*, proficiency in terrace farming, fibre working and construction – all of which they achieved in a hostile mountainous environment. That's Inca-redible.

⟨ **MAYAN MYTHOLOGY** ⟩

Featuring a large number of deities and supernatural beings, Mayan mythology anthropomorphized natural forces and phenomena in an attempt to explain where these things came from. Despite being much older, Mayan mythology shares some similarities with Aztec, for example the god Kukulkan (Quetzalcoatl to the Aztecs). The idea that the gods made multiple attempts at creating humanity is also something we'll see again with the Aztecs.

We don't have many remaining texts from the Maya peoples as so much was destroyed by the conquistadors in the Spanish colonization of the Americas. The *Popol Vuh* ("Book of the Community") is one of the only texts we have that describes Mayan myth. It comes from the K'iche' people (one of the Maya peoples) and recounts a creation myth and the exploits of the Hero Twins (who we'll get to in a bit). Originally passed down orally, the *Popol Vuh* was eventually written down by a Spanish friar in around 1550 CE.

CREATION

Here is creation, according to the *Popol Vuh*.

A troupe of creator deities, including Heart of Sky (also called Huracan), the feathered serpent Q'uq'umatz and five others, created the earth together. To separate the land from the sky, they formed a great tree which would hold the two apart. Then they created plants. But things were quiet. Too quiet.

The gods decided to create animals. But these animals did not worship the gods. Something had gone wrong – let's try again. Second time round, the gods created the first humans from mud. But these humans didn't have souls and also didn't worship the gods. So the gods destroyed what they had created. Take three: the gods created more humans from wood. Still the people did not worship the gods, so the gods washed them away in a great flood.

At last, the gods tried using maize. Maize was a precious, life-giving substance and, finally, these humans satisfied the gods. If at first you don't succeed...

GODS OF MAYAN MYTHOLOGY

These are some of the most important deities in the Mayan pantheon.

Kukulkan is a feathered serpent deity, sometimes equated with Q'uq'umatz who we met in the K'iche' creation myth as one of the group of creator gods. He is also roughly equivalent to Quetzalcoatl of Aztec mythology, who we'll encounter in due course. Kukulkan has also been identified as the Vision Serpent, a creature prominent in Mayan art, who acts as the messenger between the Maya peoples and the gods and ancestors.

Chaac is the god of rain. He is humanoid with reptilian scales and long fangs, and he carries a lightning axe with which he brings forth rain and storms. He was thought of as having four different aspects or personalities, which corresponded with the four cardinal directions. According to one myth, Chaac gave maize to the people by splitting open the mountain where all the maize was hidden with his axe.

Itzamna, as ruler of the heavens, day and night, is one of the most important Mayan deities. Depending on who you ask, Itzamna is either the son or manifestation of the creator god Hunab Ku. As a culture hero (a figure who instructs humanity or brings aspects of civilization such as traditions and culture), Itzamna is credited with teaching humans how to grow maize and how to write, as well as bringing medicine, the calendar and religious rituals to them. He is sometimes associated with the sun.

Ixchel is the goddess of the moon, midwifery, medicine and womanly crafts. She is sometimes described as the wife of Itzamna, sometimes as a manifestation of him, but she isn't always as benevolent as him. She could cause destructive floods and storms if she felt like it. Ixchel is often depicted as an aged woman with jaguar ears or other jaguar features.

THE HERO TWINS

The *Popol Vuh* story of the Hero Twins actually begins with *another* set of twins, Hun Hunahpu and Vucub Hunahpu. These boys played ball games noisily and boisterously, with no regard for the neighbours. Unfortunately, their neighbours were the Lords of Death, gods of the underworld Xibalba. "Keep it down!" one of them bellowed. The others tutted. "Pesky teenagers... No respect..."

The Lords of Death invited the twins to Xibalba and set them some tricky tests. They disguised themselves as wooden mannequins and tried to get the twins to sit on a burning bench. The twins disgraced themselves by not recognizing which were the real Lords of Death and which were wooden (embarrassing), and by sitting on the burning bench. Ouch.

The punishment for failure was death. Hun Hunahpu was decapitated, and his head was hung in a tree. When the goddess Xquic walked by, Hun Hunahpu's skull spat into her hand, impregnating her. In time, Xquic gave birth to two bouncing baby boys: Hunahpu and Xbalanque. They were the Hero Twins.

One day, Hunahpu and Xbalanque found their father's old ball game equipment, and began playing. They proved just as talented – and just as noisy – as their father. Once again, the Lords of Death were disgruntled, and summoned the twins to Xibalba.

They tried the same old tricks on Hunahpu and Xbalanque. But these twins were quick-witted. They sent mosquitoes to bite the Lords of Death, so they could tell which were real and which were wooden. They refused to sit on the burning bench because why would you sit on a burning bench?

The only way to settle it was a ball game. The Lords of Death once again tried to pull a fast one by using a ball laced with blades, but the twins eventually beat them fair and square.

The punishment for victory was death. Hey, the Lords of Death were sore losers. They demanded that the twins be burned to death. But the Hero Twins would eventually be reincarnated in the great cycle of life and death.

∽ **AZTEC MYTHOLOGY** ∽

Like the Maya peoples, the Aztecs boasted an extensive pantheon of gods, and their myths were also concerned with the creation of the world, the development of humankind and the origin of natural phenomena. As a conglomeration of many peoples and cultures, the Aztecs had many different versions and variations of their myths: they had several creation myths, for example, and there are at least four or five accounts of Quetzalcoatl's birth.

Blood sacrifice was central to Aztec mythology and religion. The Aztecs believed that sacrifices of human blood were necessary to feed the earth and prevent it from devouring everything (see Cipactli). Sacrifices were also a way of honouring or sustaining the gods: there's a myth here in which the god Huitzilopochtli must receive human blood in order to keep his strength up – you'll see.

As well as all that blood, the following pages will treat you with a delightfully destructive god called Tezcatlipoca, a guy with 401 vengeful siblings, and a *Romeo and Juliet* for Aztec times.

THE FOUR TEZCATLIPOCAS

From the void of nothingness, the first deity, Ometeotl, came into being. They were both male and female, light and dark, day and night, and good and evil. Ometeotl gave life to four children, one presiding over each of the four cardinal directions. For north: the black god Tezcatlipoca, god of night and discord. For east: the red god Xipe Totec, of gold and agriculture. For south: the blue god Huitzilopochtli, of war. And for west: the white god Quetzalcoatl, of light, life and wisdom. Together, they were the Tezcatlipocas.

The four Tezcatlipocas set to work creating the world. But there was one problem: as soon as something was created, it was consumed by the monstrous crocodile Cipactli, who was *always* hungry (Cipactli, we've all been there). So Quetzalcoatl and Tezcatlipoca hatched a plan. Tezcatlipoca lured Cipactli to the surface of the water, where Cipactli promptly ate his leg as an afternoon snack. The other gods captured Cipactli, killed him, and created the land from his dead body.

Cipactli's snack attacks were over.

THE FIVE SUNS

The Tezcatlipocas created people and more gods, including Tlaloc, god of rain, and Chalchiuhtlicue, goddess of oceans. But they lacked a sun. Tezcatlipoca volunteered to take on this task, but a jealous Quetzalcoatl knocked him out of the sky. In retaliation, Tezcatlipoca destroyed humanity with his army of jaguars.

The gods created new humans and Quetzalcoatl took over as the second sun. But the people grew disrespectful toward the gods, so Tezcatlipoca turned them into monkeys. Tlaloc became the third sun. Things were great until Tezcatlipoca seduced Tlaloc's wife (what is *wrong* with this guy?), and Tlaloc rained fire down on the earth in despair, destroying everything.

Chalchiuhtlicue was the fourth sun. She bestowed kindness on humankind, but Tezcatlipoca accused her of only *pretending* to be nice (dude, seriously?!). Devastated, Chalchiuhtlicue wept blood for 52 years, flooding the entire world. Enough was enough. Quetzalcoatl retrieved the bones of all the perished humans from the underworld and resurrected the human race. The humans emerged, blinking, into the light of the fifth and current sun, Huitzilopochtli.

HUITZILOPOCHTLI

In one tradition, Quetzalcoatl (along with his twin brother Xolotl) was actually the son of the mother goddess Coatlicue. But Coatlicue's existing children – 400 sons and one daughter, Coyolxauhqui – weren't too thrilled with their new siblings (to be fair, little brothers *are* annoying), so they attempted to murder their mother.

But never fear! The fully formed sun god Huitzilopochtli burst from his mother's womb and decapitated Coyolxauhqui, flinging her head into the sky to become the moon. He also killed many of his brothers, who were scattered across the sky as stars. All in a day's work.

But the murdered siblings (or their heads, at least) weren't finished with Huitzilopochtli yet, pursuing him in a never-ending chase. And so the sun, moon and stars chase each other across the sky each and every day.

To strengthen and nourish Huitzilopochtli in his flight, the Aztecs must offer blood sacrifices, because if Huitzilopochtli ever tires, Coyolxauhqui and her brothers will catch him and destroy the world.

QUETZALCOATL

We've already heard two accounts of Quetzalcoatl's birth – either he was the son of the first deity Ometeotl or the mother goddess Coatlicue. But those aren't the only stories. One tradition has him being the son of goddess Chimalman, born after the god Onteol appeared to her in a dream *or* after the god Mixcoatl shot an arrow between her legs *or* after she swallowed a precious gemstone. Keep up.

Quetzalcoatl's attributes are also numerous. His domains include life, light, wisdom, knowledge, arts and crafts (glue sticks at the ready), merchants, wind, dawn and the Aztec priesthood. He was many things to many people.

Quetzalcoatl is also identified with the Morning Star. A spiteful Tezcatlipoca (it's always him, isn't it?) got Quetzalcoatl drunk, and Quetzalcoatl ended up sleeping with his sister Quetzalpetlatl. In an unusual move for a god, Quetzalcoatl actually felt immense shame at his incest, so much so that he set himself on fire, and his spirit rose into the sky to become the Morning Star.

POPOCATÉPETL AND IZTACCÍHUATL

The chief's daughter Iztaccíhuatl had eyes for one man only: the warrior Popocatépetl. Popocatépetl sought Iztaccíhuatl's father's permission to marry. Sadly, dad wasn't keen on the match, so he sent Popocatépetl off to war, promising that he could marry Iztaccíhuatl if and when he returned. Popocatépetl was bound to die, right? It was a war after all.

Soon enough, news spread that Popocatépetl had been slain in battle. Overcome with shock and grief, Iztaccíhuatl collapsed and died. But, in a Shakespearean twist, it turned out that Popocatépetl's death was fake news. He was very much alive, and was heading home.

When Popocatépetl learned of Iztaccíhuatl's death, he was distraught. How could he go on living without his beloved? He built a funerary pyramid and carried Iztaccíhuatl's body to the top, before kneeling down to watch over her. The gods were so moved that they transformed the lovers into the great volcanoes that still carry their names today. And so Popocatépetl and Iztaccíhuatl's love was immortalized.

⌒☙ INCA MYTHOLOGY ☙⌒

These days, Inca civilization is probably most famous for Machu Picchu. This Inca citadel was abandoned during the Spanish conquest in the sixteenth century and wasn't rediscovered until the twentieth century. And it wasn't the only thing the Incas lost. Inca records were mostly destroyed by the conquistadors, so the evidence we have for Inca myths mostly comes from archaeology and the surviving stories of the native peoples of the Andes.

Of the utmost importance to the Incas was the sun, which was seen as giving and sustaining life. Worship of the sun god Inti was encouraged, and the central city of the empire, Cuzco, was built in Inti's honour.

The Incas used mythology to claim that they had the right to rule over the other peoples in their empire. Some myths depicted the Incas as superior to other peoples, thus justifying their elite position of authority. Later, after the empire was colonized, Inca myths were used to maintain Inca identity and beliefs in the face of Spanish rule.

VIRACOCHA

It all began with darkness. Then, the great creator god Viracocha rose from Lake Titicaca. He created the sun, moon and stars, then decided to create beings to inhabit the earth. He breathed life into the stones on the ground, which awoke as the first people.

But these people were bumbling, brainless brutes, too big and too stupid for their own good. Viracocha was, quite frankly, disgusted with them. In typical creator god fashion, he sent a great flood to destroy this first batch of people, and they were all washed away.

But second time's a charm, right? This time, Viracocha chose smaller stones, pebbles really, to breathe life into. He scattered his new pebble people all across the world. Then he equipped them with language, music, skills, clothing and crops, before walking into the Pacific Ocean, never to be seen again.

But some believe that Viracocha chose to walk the earth disguised as a beggar, guiding his creations and teaching them the ways of civilization.

INTI

As far as the Inca people were concerned, Viracocha was remote and distant. But his son Inti, the sun god, was much more relevant to the day-to-day goings on of the Inca Empire. Huge significance was placed on the sun – after all, it was essential for agriculture, and the Incas also believed that the sun was responsible for bringing rain. This made Inti the most important of the Inca gods.

Inti shone bright with his golden disc face framed by a mane of flaming rays of light. He was married to his older sister (typical), Mama Quilla the moon goddess. As patron of marriage and the menstrual cycle, Mama Quilla was seen as a mother goddess and a protector and defender of women.

The emperor of the Inca Empire, called the Sapa Inca, was considered to be the son of Inti (or "the son of the sun"). Thus the Sapa Inca could connect himself firmly with this most prominent of Inca gods.

GODS OF INCA MYTHOLOGY

Like the Romans, the Incas assimilated deities from the cultures they ruled, allowing these cultures to continue following their own gods and religions. This is why some of the gods and goddesses listed below share attributes and characteristics.

MAMA PACHA	The mother earth goddess, presiding over farming and harvesting, and second in importance only to Inti.
PACHA KAMAQ	The dragon husband of Mama Pacha, often conflated with Viracocha.
SAPAY	The god of death, and ruler of the Ukhu Pacha (underworld).
MAMA QUCHA	The goddess of the sea and fish; protector of fishermen and sailors.
MAMA SARA	The goddess of grain and corn, the staple food of the Incas.
ILLAPA	The god of the weather, who kept the galaxy in a jug and used it to make rain.
APU	Gods or spirits of mountains. Each mountain had its own Apu.
KON	The god of rain and southern wind.
URCUCHILLAY	The llama god who watched over animals.
AXOMAMMA	The goddess of potatoes. Best. God. Ever.

MANCO CAPAC

Manco Capac was the legendary founder of the Inca people and the city of Cuzco, the centre of the Inca Empire. There are two main accounts of how he founded Cuzco, and here's one of them.

Inti was dissatisfied. The people of the earth were grossly uncivilized, wearing animal skins and foraging for food. So he sent his son and daughter, Manco Capac and Mama Ocllo, to sort things out.

Inti gave his children a golden staff, telling them that wherever the staff sank completely into the ground, that was where they should build a sacred city of the sun. So Manco Capac and Mama Ocllo set out on their mission, travelling far and wide across the mountains. Eventually they came to a valley where their golden staff sank easily into the ground.

It was here that Manco Capac built a temple dedicated to his father Inti, gathered together all the people nearby and founded a magnificent city: Cuzco.

CUZCO

Cuzco was the capital city of the Inca Empire and its political and military centre. Thanks to this, Cuzco also had enormous mythological significance.

Because of the legend of Manco Capac, the people of Cuzco could claim descendancy from Inti, the most important and influential Inca god. This gave the Inca people (who originated in Cuzco) legitimacy to rule over the other peoples and cultures they assimilated into their empire. This was crucial since the Incas (those that had the special status of "Inca by blood") numbered less than 50,000 in an empire of millions.

The legendary temple said to have been built by Manco Capac was the Coricancha. Only the original foundations survive today, as the rest was destroyed when the Spanish conquistadors took Cuzco. But it would have been a sight to behold, with golden walls, a giant sun disc and a courtyard filled with golden statues. It was a symbol of the magnificence of Inti, Cuzco and the Inca people.

OCEANIA

Things are about to get watery as we sail to Oceania. First stop, Australia.

There are hundreds of different Aboriginal Australian groups, and they have inhabited Australia for more than 50,000 years. Only in the last couple of hundred years have they begun to identify themselves as a single group, although this is not universal across all Aboriginal peoples.

There is a wide variety of traditions and customs across the Aboriginal Australians, including over 300 languages, but a common thread across these various cultures is a deep reverence for the land and nature. Ceremonies play an important role in maintaining these spiritual beliefs and asserting Aboriginal identity. Art is also a fundamental aspect of Aboriginal cultures: Aboriginal art is the oldest unbroken art tradition in the world and includes rock painting, wood carving, textile work, basket weaving and the more contemporary dot painting. Aboriginal Australians also have a strong music tradition, featuring instruments such as the didgeridoo.

The neighbouring Māori people of New Zealand developed entirely separately from the Aboriginal Australians. Originally sailing from Polynesia, the first Māori settled in New Zealand in multiple waves in the first half of the fourteenth century. Over the course of the next few hundred years, they developed their own culture and identity before the first Europeans landed on their soil in the eighteenth century. Māori now make up around 16.5 per cent of New Zealand's population, and traditional Māori culture has experienced a revival in recent years, following widespread suppression of Māori identity by European settlers throughout the nineteenth century.

Integral parts of Māori culture include *moko* tattoos, *whakairo* wood carving, music and dance. Māori are well represented in New Zealand's sporting culture. Rugby fans will be familiar with the haka performed by the All Blacks before a match – this dance originates from Māori culture and is almost always led by a member of the team of Māori descent.

ABORIGINAL MYTHOLOGY

Aboriginal mythology stretches back for thousands of years and has been passed down orally throughout the generations. There are countless different beliefs and customs among Aboriginal Australian peoples, and this chapter can't speak for all of them. The stories told here are a snapshot of a few different peoples, and are by no means universal across Australia. This is also a living mythology, with Aboriginal Australians still telling these tales today, so by their nature these myths are fluid and variable.

One theme that is a common refrain in Aboriginal myths is the importance of nature. Many stories have a topographical focus – that is, they are concerned with the form and formation of the natural environment. By telling and listening to these stories, Aboriginal Australians learn about the geography of the land and form a close connection with the world around them as well as the ancestors who formed that world.

DREAMTIME

Key to understanding Aboriginal mythology is the concept of Dreamtime (also called the Dreaming). Broadly speaking, Dreamtime is a world view held by Aboriginal Australians, encompassing rules and morals for living a good life and upholding relationships between people, animals and the natural environment.

As part of this broader concept, Dreamtime is also the era before the world existed, during which everything we know was created. Spiritual beings and ancestors roamed a formless space, creating all the features of the earth such as mountains and rivers. These Dreaming stories are fundamental to Aboriginal mythology, often providing environmental understanding, like the phases of the moon, and moral guidance, like showing respect toward animals.

SONGLINES

The routes of the ancestors who travelled across the world during Dreamtime are called songlines or dreaming tracks. Aboriginal Australians historically used these songlines to navigate the land, reaching important natural features and resources, and encountering other

Aboriginal peoples. Today, these songlines continue to connect Aboriginal Australians to their ancestors and the land.

Sometimes, songlines are used in the rite of passage called walkabout or temporary mobility, which is undertaken by adolescent boys. A boy must survive in the wilderness for several months, using songlines to navigate and to reach out to spiritual guides. When he returns, he is a man.

One major songline is the Tjilbruke Dreaming Track along Gulf St Vincent on Australia's south coast. Tjilbruke was a creator ancestor of the Kaurna people. He carried the body of his nephew along the coast after he was killed for unlawfully killing an emu. Along the way, Tjilbruke's tears formed six freshwater springs and eventually, wearied by the journey and his grief, Tjilbruke transformed into a glossy ibis.

THE RAINBOW SERPENT

The Rainbow Serpent is a creator deity that features, under different names, in Aboriginal myths across all of Australia.

In Dreamtime, before the world was created, everything was barren and formless. But when the time came, the Rainbow Serpent burst forth from underneath the earth, and as she pushed upward she formed ridges and mountains. She began her journey across the world. Since she could control water, she filled the land with rivers and lakes, and these waters caused all the plants to spring up. Then the Rainbow Serpent brought life to the earth, creating animals and people.

The Rainbow Serpent watched over and protected the humans. But sometimes they disobeyed her laws, and she was forced to punish them with drought or flood. She could bring destruction as well as creation.

The Rainbow Serpent made her home in the waterholes scattered across the land. And whenever you see a rainbow, it is the Rainbow Serpent herself moving between two waterholes, creating a great arc across the sky.

HERE COMES THE SUN

In many Aboriginal myths, the sun appears as a female deity. Here are two examples.

Wuriunpranilli originates from northern Australia. Every morning she lights a small fire in the east: this is dawn. She covers herself with red ochre, creating a stunning sunrise. Then she journeys into the sky, and the birds break out singing, waking the humans. Wuriunpranilli's journey takes all day, but eventually she reaches the west. Her red ochre is long gone, so she reapplies it, causing a vibrant sunset. Then she travels through the earth toward the east, in time for the next morning.

Gnowee comes from the Wotjobaluk people. When all the world was dark and food was scarce, Gnowee left her infant son one day to search for yams, using only a torch to light her way. This search took her so far that she lost her son. She climbed into the sky to get a better look, and there she remains to this day, eternally searching with her torch for her lost child.

CROW STEALS FIRE

Crow watched a group of seven sisters as they cooked their yams with their funny glowing sticks. Those yams looked *delicious*. Crow simply had to get hold of those glowing sticks, so he came up with a plan.

Crow tricked the sisters into disturbing an ant hill which had snakes hidden inside. Unsurprisingly, the snakes attacked the sisters, and the sisters were forced to use their glowing sticks to fend them off. But the sticks weren't made for combat, and they broke apart. The glowing parts fell off and rolled toward Crow. They were pieces of coal! That must be the secret to cooking. Crow seized the coals and ran off.

Now that Crow had unlocked the secret of fire, it wasn't long before he attracted a huge crowd of animals all demanding that he cook for them. Crow grew sick of their noise, so he flung the red-hot coals at them all. But all this did was start a raging bushfire which burnt Crow's feathers.

And that's why the crow is black.

THE THREE BROTHERS

There were once three brothers who embarked on their walkabout ritual. But they soon grew worried about their parents (who, quite honestly, were probably enjoying the peace and quiet), so the youngest brother volunteered to check on them. As he was leaving the camp, he spotted a witch. "Ah, don't worry," he said to himself, "it's only a witch."

He checked on his parents and travelled back to the camp. But his brothers had vanished, and in their place stood the witch. The youngest brother demanded to know what she had done with his brothers. "I ate them," she replied. "And now I'm going to eat YOU!"

But before she had the chance, the youngest brother struck her with his boomerang, and she dropped down dead. He gathered up his brothers' bones and buried them. Then, so distraught that he'd been unable to save his brothers, he killed himself.

The spirits transformed the bodies into three great mountains, which still stand today – the Three Brothers mountains in New South Wales.

THE SEVEN SISTERS

We met the seven sisters briefly when Crow stole fire from them. Here is a different story about them.

The seven sisters were – quite frankly – minding their own business, when suddenly a wild man appeared out of nowhere and started chasing them. He kept yelling that he was in love with them and wanted to marry one of them, and would just *not* take no for an answer. The sisters kept running and running, but the man kept chasing and chasing.

Eventually, one of the sisters got tired and stopped for a drink. As she drank from a pool, she heard a noise behind her. She whipped her head round. The man was approaching her, licking his lips. She started running again, as fast as she could.

She caught up with her sisters, but what now? It seemed the man would never stop pursuing them. In a desperate attempt to escape him, they launched themselves into the sky, becoming the Pleiades or Seven Sisters constellation.

⌒∾ MĀORI MYTHOLOGY ∾⌒

Having settled in New Zealand after voyaging from Polynesia, the Māori grew their mythology out of Polynesian myths and beliefs. The Polynesians were great navigators of the ocean, so it's no surprise that many of their myths and narratives feature themes of the sea, water and travel. This has been passed down into Māori mythology as well. Māori mythology also focuses on the origins of natural phenomena, human nature and cultural practices, such as fire, death and art.

Like Aboriginal mythology, Māori mythology is an oral tradition. One key aspect of this is the reciting of *whakapapa*, a person's individual genealogy and lineage. This framework binds Māori people to their history and their land, and so, through *whakapapa*, both the origins of the world and the place of the Māori within it are explained.

In the next few pages, you'll meet a grumpy sea god, a very patient fire goddess, and the great Māori hero Maui, who goes on many adventures and meets an unfortunate end.

RANGI AND PAPA

Ranginui and Papatūānuku (aka Rangi and Papa) are another sky-father and earth-mother pairing, playing the lead roles in this Māori creation myth.

Rangi and Papa were *really* into each other. They lay in the darkness, pressed tightly together, and Papa bore Rangi countless sons. But these sons were all trapped in the middle of their parents' tight embrace, unable to move or even see, since no light could reach them.

The brothers wanted to break free from their parents, but, like all siblings, they bickered about how to go about it. Tūmatauenga, the god of war, proposed killing Rangi and Papa, but Tāne-mahuta, god of forests, had an altogether more peaceful idea: separate them.

Each of the brothers in turn tried to prise Rangi and Papa apart, with no luck. It was down to Tāne-mahuta to sort everything out again. Using his immensely strong legs, Tāne-mahuta pushed Rangi up into the sky, separating him from his wife Papa, the earth below.

THE FAMILY OF TANGAROA

When Rangi and Papa were torn apart, their son Tāwhirimātea was *livid*. He alone out of his brothers had not agreed to the separation, and you bet he was going to do something about it. As god of storms, he whipped up a ferocious hurricane that destroyed his brother Tāne-mahuta's forests and drove his brother Tangaroa into the ocean.

Now forced to hide in the seas, Tangaroa fathered a son. Punga was the ancestor of all strange and deformed creatures (the insult "offspring of Punga" means an ugly person – ouch), and he himself had two sons: Ikatere and Tū-te-wehiwehi. These two sons were so terrified of Tāwhirimātea's continued onslaught against their family, that Ikatere fled to the ocean, becoming the ancestor of all fish, and Tū-te-wehiwehi fled to the forests, becoming the ancestor of all reptiles.

Tangaroa still holds a grudge against his brother Tāne-mahuta for harbouring Tū-te-wehiwehi, whose rightful ancestral home is the ocean. And for this reason, the Māori consider the land and the sea opposing realms.

THE FIRST HUMANS

Here are two accounts of the creation of humans.

One tale identifies Tāne-mahuta as humankind's creator. He created the first human, Hineahuone, out of soil and clay. Then he coupled with her (jeez, give her a minute to adjust to being alive) and Hineahuone gave birth to a daughter: Hinetītama. Tāne-mahuta fathered numerous offspring with Hinetītama as well, and they inhabited the land. Eventually, Hinetītama discovered that her husband was also her father and fled to the underworld in shame, renaming herself Hine-nui-te-pō.

In another story, the first man Tiki was so lonely that when he saw his reflection in a pool he convinced himself it was a companion. He dived in, but the image shattered. Tiki then covered the pool with soil, and the pool brought forth the first woman. This woman caught sight of an eel and became... excited, and Tiki mirrored her excitement, resulting in the first ever sexual act. Tiki now lends his name, through distortion by Westerners, to tiki culture and tiki bars.

THE ORIGIN OF *WHAKAIRO*

Once, a young boy called Te Manuhauturuki sailed too far from land and was captured by Tangaroa. Te Manuhauturuki's father Ruatepupuke went searching for his son. He came to Tangaroa's underwater house, which was covered with intricate wooden carvings. There, Ruatepupuke saw his beloved boy, transformed into a wooden figure and displayed like a trophy. Ruatepupuke was filled with anguish. Tangaroa must pay.

Ruatepupuke filled all the cracks and crevices of the house to block out the light. Then he hid himself by the porch. Tangaroa's fish descendants returned to the house and fell asleep. But when morning came, they did not wake, since inside the house it was still dark.

This was Ruatepupuke's chance. He set Tangaroa's house ablaze. Some of the fish – the flying fish and the mullet – were able to escape, but many more were not so lucky. Ruatepupuke fled the scene, carrying with him his wooden son and some other carvings, bringing the art of carving, *whakairo*, to the people.

MAUI GOES FISHING

The demigod hero Maui has experienced some recent popularity thanks to his appearance in the much-loved Disney film *Moana*.

Maui's older brothers never let him go fishing with them because they were big meanies. But Maui had a plan. He enhanced his fishing line with a Māori incantation, then hid in his brothers' canoe.

When they were out at sea, Maui leaped from his hiding place and, with much bravado, promised to catch the biggest fish *ever*. He attached his fish hook, made from his grandmother's jawbone (hope she didn't mind), onto his fishing line and cast it out. And sure enough, it went taut. Heaving as hard as he could, Maui pulled in the biggest fish imaginable. It was as big as, say, the North Island of New Zealand, which is indeed what it became. The canoe, meanwhile, became the South Island.

These two islands are still known as Te Ika-a-Māui (the fish of Maui) and Te Waka-a-Māui (the canoe of Maui). What can Maui say, except "you're welcome"?

MAUI AND MAHUIKA

Maui wanted to know where fire came from, so he visited his ancestor, the fire goddess Mahuika. He asked her for fire and she agreed, handing him one of her burning fingernails.

As Maui headed off, he grew curious. What would happen if he took *all* of Mahuika's fire? So he discarded the fingernail and returned to Mahuika, claiming to have dropped the fingernail in a pool. Mahuika rolled her eyes and handed him another fingernail.

Maui soon returned, claiming to have dropped this fingernail, too. Mahuika handed him another, but again he came back empty-handed. She gave him another, then another, then another, until she had given Maui all her fingernails *and* toenails except one.

Mahuika grew suspicious. Surely no one was this clumsy? She refused to hand over her last toenail, instead throwing it down and causing a raging fire. It took a great downpour of rain to extinguish it. But Mahuika saved the embers and hid them inside the trees, whose bark is still used to light fires today.

MAUI VISITS THE UNDERWORLD

Maui didn't fancy dying. He wanted immortality, and he decided to go get it from Hine-nui-te-pō, the ruling goddess of the underworld.

Taking with him a troupe of birds as his wingmen (literally), Maui travelled to the underworld. There was only one problem: the only way to achieve immortality was to enter Hine-nui-te-pō through her vagina. And there she was, asleep on her back with her legs spread. But Maui could see jagged obsidian rocks between her thighs.

Ordering the birds not to laugh lest they wake the goddess, Maui dived right in. But the sight was too ridiculous for one bird, who burst out laughing (and who can blame him?). Hine-nui-te-pō woke, felt Maui inside her, and snapped her vagina shut, crushing Maui to pieces with the sharp obsidian rocks. Thus Maui failed in his mission to bring immortality to humankind. But what a way to go.

And so death will come for us all. Just hopefully not via obsidian vagina teeth.

CONCLUSION

The mythologies in this book are some of the most vibrant out there, and they're only the beginning. There's plenty more to tuck into. If you're a fan of Hermes and Loki, for example, you could check out Anansi of the West African Akan people, or the wily Coyote of numerous Native American traditions.

Despite the diversity of cultures and beliefs, there are striking similarities between many of these tales. Snakes and dragons, for example, hold near-universal significance throughout this book, and we've encountered our fair share of floods, earth mothers, sun/moon origin stories and, yes, incestuous brother–sister relationships. These myths are attempting to answer the same big questions: where did we come from? Why do we die? And is my girlfriend a spider demon?

So, while each mythology is unique (after all, there can only ever be one Sun Wukong), isn't it amazing, and comforting, that you might be asking the same questions as someone 10,000 years ago on the other side of the globe?

With all the benefits of modern-day science, many might dismiss these myths as pure fiction. And that's a great shame. Myths are so much more than stories: they offer unparalleled insights into the lives and histories of the world's peoples, they instil people with a sense of belonging and cultural pride, they teach important lessons about respecting the earth or not shaving off people's hair for a laugh (looking at *you*, Loki), they're creative and inspiring, they're hugely influential in contemporary Western culture (superhero films, *The Lord of the Rings*, *Assassin's Creed* and *God of War*... none of these exist in a vacuum), and, above all, they're really good fun. There's nothing fictional about any of that.

FURTHER READING

Berresford Ellis, Peter, *The Mammoth Book of Celtic Myths and Legends* (Little, Brown, 2003)

Buxton, Richard, *The Complete World of Greek Mythology* (Thames & Hudson, 2004)

Chinese Myths and Folk Tales (Barnes & Noble, 2020)

Dalley, Stephanie (trans.), *Myths from Mesopotamia* (Oxford University Press, 2008)

Daniels, Mark, *World Mythology in Bite-sized Chunks* (Michael O'Mara Books, 2016)

Doniger, Wendy, *Hindu Myths* (Penguin, 2004)

Fry, Stephen, *Mythos* (Penguin, 2017)
- *Heroes* (Penguin, 2018)
- *Troy* (Penguin, 2020)

Gaiman, Neil, *Norse Mythology* (W. W. Norton & Company, 2017)

Hamilton, Edith, *Mythology: Timeless Tales of Gods and Heroes* (Little, Brown, 2011)

Leeming, David, *The Oxford Companion to World Mythology* (Oxford University Press, 2009)

Orbell, Margaret, *The Illustrated Encyclopedia of Māori Myth and Legend* (Canterbury University Press, 1995)

Pinch, Geraldine, *Egyptian Mythology: A Guide to the Gods, Goddesses, and Traditions of Ancient Egypt* (Oxford University Press, 2004)

Read, Kay Almere & Gonzalez, Jason J., *Mesoamerican Mythology* (Oxford University Press, 2002)

Tales of Japan (Chronicle Books, 2019)

Wilkinson, Richard H., *The Complete Gods and Goddesses of Ancient Egypt* (Thames & Hudson, 2017)

Have you enjoyed this book?
If so, why not write a review on
your favourite website?

If you're interested in finding out more about
our books, find us on Facebook at **Summersdale
Publishers**, on Twitter at **@Summersdale**
and on Instagram at **@summersdalebooks**
and get in touch. We'd love to hear from you!

Thanks very much for buying
this Summersdale book.

WWW.SUMMERSDALE.COM

Image Credits